Leaving Long Island
...and other departures

Fern Kupfer

A Memoir

Culicidae
PRESS, LLC
culicidaepress.com

Ames | Berlin | Gainesville | Rome

Culicidae Press, LLC
918 5th Street
Ames, IA 50010
USA
www.culicidaepress.com

editor@culicidaepress.com

Ames | Berlin | Gainesville | Rome

LEAVING LONG ISLAND …AND OTHER DEPARTURES. Copyright © 2012 by Fern Kupfer. All rights reserved.

For more information about the author go to www.fernkupfer.com

Parts of this book were previously published in: *Before and After Zachariah* by Fern Kupfer (Academy Chicago Press, 3rd edition, 1998); "Sleepwalking Through Suburbia," in *Nice Jewish Girls: Growing up in America*, edited by Marlene Adler Marks (Plume Penguin, 1996); "Trust," in *Mirror, Mirror on the Wall: Women Writers Explore Their Favorite Fairy Tales*, edited by Kate Bernheimer (Anchor Books, 1998); "Another Traditional Arab-Jewish Iowa Potluck," in *Swaying: Essays on Inter-cultural Love*, edited by Jessie Carroll Grearson and Lauren B. Smith (University of Iowa Press, 1995)

No part of this book may be reproduced in any form by any electronic or mechanized means (including photocopying, recording, or information storage and retrieval) without written permission, except in the case of brief quotations embodied in critical articles and reviews.

Respect copyrights, encourage creativity!

For more information please visit www.culicidaepress.com

ISBN: 978-1479219278

Cover design and interior layout © 2012 by polytekton.com

Dedication

For Barbara (forever and ever and ever)

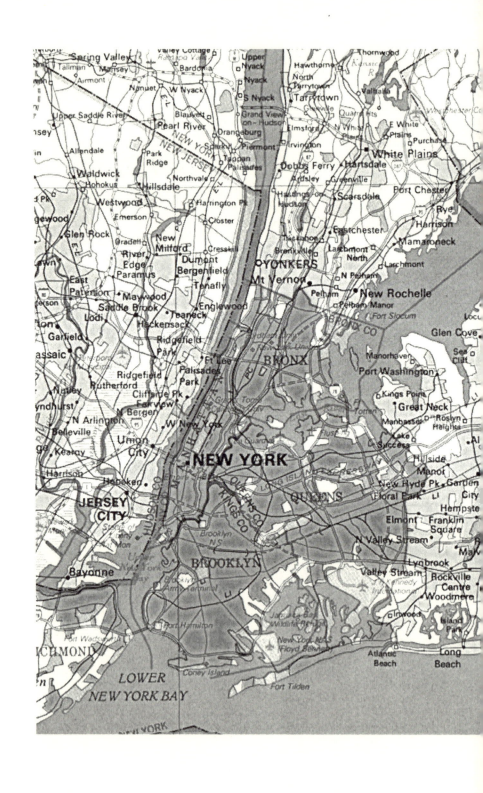

Plainview High School Graduation, 1964

Prologue

My first husband once called me "emotionally promiscuous." This was in defense of his more ordinary promiscuity. He thought I became intimate too easily with everyone; I shared too much and encouraged others to do the same. A more charitable explanation is that I am open and interested in people.

I was thinking about this as the woman and I told each other practically our whole life stories. She was seated next to me on a plane going from Des Moines to La Guardia. She looked to be in her forties, dark-eyed and pretty, dressed professionally in a tailored black suit and heels. First there was small talk about the weather for flying (good) and the plane being exactly on time (amazing). She told me she was going to a radiology conference. I told her I was going to Long Island for my high school reunion. "What fun," she said.

I was going to stay in Great Neck with my best friend, Barbara, one of the planners on the reunion committee who vowed after organizing the 20th that she was never, never, never going to do it again. Barbara was a high school cheerleader and had been voted "Most Versatile" Senior Celebrity, Plainview class of 1964. Part of her versatility included changing her mind.

Barbara and I have been friends since junior high when she invited herself over and then slept at my house practically every weekend through high school. She had a tumultuous home life with a mother prone to emotional outbursts and a stepfather who was unreasonably strict. My peaceful, happy house was her sanctuary. Together over the years, Barbara and I have shared secrets and college apartments; we've been together through marriages and divorces, the births of our children, the deaths of our parents. Life. Or, as Zorba says: The Whole Catastrophe!

Now we are grandmothers. Barbara's kids have remained living in New York. My daughter Gabi and her family are in Chicago, where I regularly make the trip from Iowa. My granddaughter was four, almost the age of reason, when her brother Wilson was born. "I'm not jealous," Ruthie said, on her first visit to the hospital to see her new brother. "I'm not jealous," she would repeat, as if to convince herself.

I look at my grandchildren, both of them in school now, and think how their sweet babyhoods were over in a blink. They are themselves already. Yet sometimes I imagine them in full adulthood, working at jobs, becoming parents themselves. They will have lives I will not be witness to.

To them I am Grandma Fern. At first, this descriptor seemed unreal. Shouldn't I be fatter? Smell like lavender talcum and chicken soup? It was as if I were play-acting, trying on the new role. It was the same feeling I had when, at twenty-one, I married and first uttered the words "my husband" to describe the person who had been my boyfriend for so long. I was a *wife*. A few years later, I recall seeing my body swollen in pregnancy and knowing I was going to be someone's *mother*. A child might yell "mommy" across a crowded room and could be calling me. And later I was always introduced as *Zachariah's mother*, as having a "special" child defined me for so long. I was a *stepmother*, too. The evil stepmother, my girls used to say, sometimes only half in jest. I remember the first time a student knocked on my office door and addressed me as *professor*. Last week, I went out for lunch with a friend whose husband recently died; she finds comfort in sleeping on his side of the king-sized bed. "I hate that word: '*Widow*,'" she told me. *Two senior citizens*, my husband says now when we go to the movies.

Our lives most often surprise us. Just as we get used to being who we are, we become someone else again.

After the woman on the plane told me she was attending a radiology conference, our conversation turned to cancer detection. It was then I revealed I had been recently diagnosed with the BRCA gene for hereditary breast and ovarian cancer. In a few weeks, I would be making some difficult decisions about having preventative surgery.

The woman shook her head. Yes, she was familiar with the BRCA gene; she had survived her own cancer, a colon cancer that appeared when she was only in her thirties. She had three little girls and worried about the genetic component. Though she believed having cancer made her a better, more grateful mother.

She told me her daughters had names beginning with the letter "M," though she did not plan that. I told her that both of my husbands were named Joe, though I had not planned that either. We opened up our wallets. I showed her a photo of my grandchildren and my daughter Gabi. "She looks just like you," the woman said.

"She doesn't really," I said, smiling. This has become something of a joke between Gabi and me. "Mom, it's really rude if someone tells you we look alike and you say we don't. It's insulting." Gabi has counseled me to respond affirmatively: "Yes, a lot of people tell us we look alike."

The truth is that, feature for feature, there are few similarities. But there is the smile, the stance, and something ineffable echoing through the generations. And maybe the genetic predisposition to cancer.

"Girls are complicated and wonderful," I said to my seatmate who has shown me a photograph of her three, brown-eyed daughters. I have raised two stepdaughters, Megan and Katie, now adults, who are complicated and wonderful.

"You also had only girls?" my seat-mate asked.

Sometime after the thrilling New York skyline came into view, I told her about Zachariah, my beautiful, damaged boy. It's hard to compress the love and loss of Zachariah in any meaningful way, especially to someone you have just met. "He had a rare syndrome. Also with a genetic component," I said. The plane noises seemed unnaturally quiet when I added: "He passed away just after he was sixteen."

"Oh, I'm so sorry," the woman said.

"He was in a wonderful, loving facility," I said, just to show that I was all right. "I was very grateful for his care."

Soon we landed and coasted to the gate; we unbuckled, rose gingerly and stretched. In the aisle, passengers tugged stuffed baggage from the overhead compartments and then slowly filed out of the plane. *Bye-bye. Bye now. Bye-bye.* The flight attendant gave her little baby bye-byes. I walked through the jetway, stiff, after sitting for so long. I was eager with anticipation, not having seen Barbara in more than a year. My seatmate, whose name I did not know, walked ahead. In a week's time, I would not recognize her in a crowd. Odds are, I will never see her again. Yet we knew such personal details about each other's lives. Strangers on a plane. Everyone has a story. Here's mine.

1

Looking backward to Plainview, Long Island, this is what I see through the filter of memory: There is an adolescent girl spinning in the circle of her friends; her pink bedroom with the ruffled curtains; the phone is ringing, usually for her. She is safe, but slightly bored, looking dreamily beyond the horizon of the next shopping center and waiting for her real life to begin.

Time meanders, a crazy river, but I'll start here: When I was ten years old, my parents, younger brother and I moved to Plainview, Long Island. It was 1956 and getting out of "the City" was something parents wanted to do for their children—fresh air, grass, better schools. Long Island was the Promised Land for my parents' generation.

In suburbia in the fifties and early sixties, we had it good. Never before had American Jews enjoyed so much financial and personal security. Look how far we had come from a tenement to a three-bedroom split-level with two-and-a-half baths. Look how far we were from the devastation of the Holocaust. How finally after assimilation, it was easy to be ourselves. From the *shtetl* to success. From pogroms to prosperity.

Suburbia seemed rural then. "Put your shoes on, Ma, we're going to town," I used to say when we picked up my father at the Long Island Railroad in Hicksville(!), New York. Wives put on fresh lipstick and moved over to the passenger's seat when the men—all in hats and dark suits, newspapers rolled up under their arms—emerged from the train.

Plainview, Long Island. I was afraid walking home from school that I wouldn't be able to find my way. All the streets looked alike. So did the houses. Suburban mothers waited in their brand new kitchens with all the latest appliances. (We had a pink General Electric refrigerator with revolving shelves.) My mother actually wore a frilly apron over her dress and had a snack ready for me. Up and down different blocks other children were similarly greeted.

After my grandmother died, my grandfather, Papa, came to live with us, having his own room in what other suburban families called *the den*. Even in winter he sat on a lawn chair in the driveway smoking a cigar, so far from the Old World.

There was my Papa sitting in the driveway of our house in Plainview; Cleo, our family's sweet-natured dog lay at his feet. She was an odd-looking spaniel/dachshund mix. When I was in junior high, we rescued her from the Bide-a-Wee, home of abandoned pups. "Roll over and I'll pet you," my grandfather commanded. Cleo obeyed, staying still until Papa got tired of rubbing her tummy. "To be in America," he would declare, "even a dog is lucky."

When Oak Drive school let out at three o'clock, Papa walked to meet me. I remember my grandfather in his long, blue overcoat, walking up Pasadena Drive, Jamaica Avenue, Oak Drive, looking like some old world Tevye lost in the maze of suburban streets. Papa met me at school to carry my books home. "*Luz mir truggin*," he'd command in Yiddish. Give it here!

I begged my mother, "'Can't you keep Papa in the house?" Apparently she could not. I walked home from sixth grade with my friends, followed by a gaunt, old Jewish man carrying a pink loose-leaf notebook.

1984: We read Orwell's novel in Mr. Colomby's high school English class and it scared the hell out of me. Those writhing, hungry rats: *Julia! Take Julia!* Mr. Colomby was also the manager to jazz great Thelonious Monk, although none of us knew who Monk was at the time. Teaching English at a suburban high school was definitely a side job, one Mr. C. did with little preparation and less interest. Often he'd go off on a tangent and talk about movies and books. He liked me because I read a lot and saw Fellini movies. Carol Kirschbaum told me that on the days I was absent he used to give the class a study hall.

2001: A Space Odyssey. I saw the movie in college and like everyone else thought it was Kubrick's masterpiece. It was a given that my friends and I smoked grass before going to the movies. *Let's get stoned and go to the movies,* we said. We sat in the parking lot behind the theatre, covertly passing a joint. About five years ago I saw *2001* on television and it was such a bore. Maybe it was because the movie didn't age well. Or because I wasn't watching it on a big screen. More likely, the movie was dull because I wasn't stoned.

In 2011, I received a social security check. Despite the gloom and doom about how the government can't make anything work right, signing up for social security was easy; the check is directly deposited in my account the third Wednesday of every month without fail. Thank you, President Roosevelt.

My mother once described where she was when she heard that President Roosevelt had died: On April 12, 1945, she was in a crowded New York city bus coming from her job as a salesgirl in Bloomingdale's. She was not yet pregnant with me because my father was on a Navy ship somewhere in the Philippines. On that day, my mother was going home to her parents' apartment in the Bronx. My mother and father had given up their own apartment while he was away at war. "Roosevelt was dead and the whole bus was crying," my mother told me. "Even the bus driver."

After Roosevelt's death, an editorial in *The New York Times* said, "Men will thank God on their knees a hundred years from now that Franklin D. Roosevelt was in the White House." Everyone in my family, my grandparents, my parents and all their friends voted for FDR and spoke about him and Eleanor Roosevelt with reverence. I never met anyone who thought otherwise until I moved to the Midwest and heard conservative Republicans who believed it was Roosevelt who set the country on the road to ruin.

And of course I recall exactly where I was when John F. Kennedy was shot. I was in Plainview High School in Mr. Maze's senior creative writing class. It was late afternoon on a Friday, the next-to-last class of the day when Mr. Gould, the principal, came on the public address system: *Our President has been shot.* Mr. Gould's voice gave meaning to the phrase "announced gravely."

So focused was I on my teenage life that for a second I thought that *our* president meant Steven Schiffman, the president of our senior class. He was a smart, skinny boy with big plans for student council fund-raising. Why in the world would anyone shoot Steven? The room sat in hushed silence. Our English teacher choked up and walked into the hall to compose himself. Mr. Maze, a passionate teacher, was my idol. He taught us to love words. He read aloud—James Joyce and Willa Cather and F. Scott Fitzgerald and Virginia Woolf—all with a sonorous FM voice that made the girls fall in love with him even though he was muckle-mouthed and had pop eyes behind thick glasses.

Once I wrote a story about a grandfather who had seen the Czar and Mr. Maze read the story to the class, making it sound a whole lot better than it was. Although my real Papa

Leaving Long Island...and other departures

had indeed seen the Czar passing through his village in a fancy carriage, the fictional grandfather died at the end of the story. This made me feel guilty since my grandfather was alive. Papa was over eighty then and so forgetful that if I stepped outside to get the mail, he locked the door. "Who is dere?" he would say with suspicion when I pounded to be let in. He'd put dirty dishes back into the cabinets, which drove my mother wild. My parents thought Papa might one day set the house on fire with his cigars. He never did, but once he drank dishwashing detergent, Pink Liquid Thrill, and then vomited up clean-smelling bubbles. "Vat vas that juice, Ruthie?" he asked my mom. "It's terrible!"

Mr. Maze told the class that my short story made him cry. That was the kind of man he was: unafraid in front of a high school class to reveal that stories had such a power over him. When I graduated, Mr. Maze took my hand and made me promise I would "never stop writing."

During the same class period, the principal came back on the PA to tell us that President Kennedy was declared dead; school would be dismissed early. My classmates went to their lockers and there was noise in the hall. A bunch of girls were happy to get out of school; they were all talking excitedly about hitting the pizza place across the street. I was crying. I remember thinking I was not "like them," although their families had probably voted for Kennedy, too. Everyone I knew had voted for our handsome, young president, even though there was some discussion about whether or not his Catholicism would pose a problem.

It was windy and blustery when my friends and I walked from school that November afternoon in 1963. We stayed home with our families Thanksgiving weekend, glued to the television. We watched John-John salute as instructed by his dazed and beautiful mother; we watched live as Jack Ruby shot the assassin, Lee Harvey Oswald. We knew then how so much could change in only one day.

After my grandfather died, the house in Plainview seemed much more traditionally suburban without an old man sitting in a lawn chair on the concrete driveway. For years afterward I had a recurring dream. I am riding a train and see my grandfather in his long, dark coat, walking up the aisle. Sometimes he is sitting by a window, reading his Jewish newspaper. "Papa?" I say, shocked, but delighted to see him. "Papa, what are you doing here?"

He barely nods in recognition. He shushes me, does not want to talk. "Go," he tells me, waving me away with this hand. "*Gai avek.*" Strange, but the dismissal does not seem unkind. *Go away. And go on with your life,* he seems to say. I always awoke missing him.

Long Island, 1964: The night before I left for college, I sat on my bed, writing in my diary. *Dear Hope.* The diary I kept in high school was "Hope." In those days, girls named their diaries—they might still. I wrote every night, expressing desires and dreams, sounding as sensitive and popular as I imagined someone reading my diary would think I was.

The summer of '64 we didn't have air-conditioning in the house on Warren Place. It was hot folding my new heather crewneck sweaters, matching knee socks and A-line wool skirts for the autumn in upstate New York. Everything was soon neatly packed in a trunk by the door. My parents were going to drive me to college. My high school best friend Barbara was also assigned to Randall Hall, although we both decided with some maturity not to room together, so we could branch out and make new friends. There were too many students crowding into the dorms that first semester; some girls had to sleep in the student lounges. I had only one roommate, but Barbara was assigned to a triple in the dorm basement. One of her roommates, a pretty blonde from a small upstate New York town, got pregnant and didn't make it back after semester break. I remember the girl crying in the stairway one weekend after her visiting boyfriend went back home.

I was still a virgin, not venturing further than make-out sessions with the boys I dated in high school. Then there was Joey, my boyfriend before he became my first husband, who offered declarations of love, pressuring me to "go all the way." I told him I wanted to go to college "still a virgin." He accepted this with resignation and some petulance.

I waited until Christmas break of my freshman year in college before we "did it." I was nominated among my new friends in the dorm, the first to offer myself up and then tell everybody what it was like. It was as if we were sacrificing a virgin. Which we were.

On New Year's Eve, the last night of 1964, I was at Joey's parents' apartment in Flushing. They were out at a party and he said they wouldn't be home until after midnight. We were in his room in a single bed; his pillowcase smelled of boy-sweat and Clearasil. On the ceiling was a picture of Willie Mays leaping into the air to catch a fly ball. I looked at the photo—*Say Hey Willie,* the fans used to call out—then closed my eyes. Intercourse didn't hurt as much as I thought it was going to, but it didn't feel great either. "This is it?" I thought. Afterward, Joey seemed so utterly grateful. We ate ice cream and cookies. One day I was a virgin. And then the next day I wasn't.

2

I want to believe that tsuris—bad luck—should be logically rationed. Oh, not her God—she already had two terrible things happen. You know about her son, Zachariah? That adorable little boy? And of course the very bad behavior of her first husband, how explosively that marriage broke apart? Enough.

"Well, this doesn't look like anything exciting to me," the surgeon said. Young, with a Midwestern, sports-guy confidence, Dr. P. was looking at the results of a second mammogram and ultra-sound. "What was it that concerned Dr. Amin?"

My husband was sitting in a plastic chair in the corner of the room. Though I'd told him it was unnecessary, he insisted on going with me to the doctor. Joe is my devoted second husband, retired, and so had time on his hands.

Yes, my internist, Dr. Rupal Amin, had been concerned. During a routine annual check-up, she felt a lump in my left breast, though less than two months earlier, my mammogram was clean. Dr. Amin is a young Indian woman whose meticulous approach to medicine includes scans and lab tests, but she is also a practitioner of meditation, yoga, nasal cleansing. Her office is decorated with hand-written instructions: *Love people and use things. Do not love things and use people.*

Lying on the table, my left arm over my head, I tried to feel what she felt: a breast which already had scars from two benign lumps removed over twenty years ago, the same year my first marriage was breaking up. Dr. Amin is very earnest, so I was reluctant to disappoint her. Still, I couldn't feel anything. "Isn't that just thickening around the old scars?" I asked.

"Hmm," she said, feeling around. 'Hmm," she said again, digging in deeper with intensity.

Because of my family history, I had anticipated that someday I would get breast cancer, although frankly, this was not as frightening as it used to be. Maybe because the kids were grown and (mostly) out on their own. Or maybe because of the medical advances. The word cancer just doesn't have the same death sentence feel as it once did.

I can name so many women—friends, colleagues, mothers of my kids' friends—who have had breast cancer, survived and thrived. My own mother's breast cancer was diagnosed when she was in her late sixties. She lived another ten years before the cancer spread to her bones.

"Had you ever considered being tested for the BRCA gene?" Dr. P. asked. I knew about the BRCA gene, a marker for early breast and ovarian cancers. "The genetics clinic is right here in the hospital. Because of your background, your insurance should cover it."

There was no ovarian cancer I knew of in my family. Both of my maternal cousins—one of whom had a recurring breast cancer—had tested negative for the BRCA gene. "Your mother had cancer after menopause," he noted. "And your maternal grandmother? How old was she when the cancer occurred?"

The age of my maternal grandmother at the time of diagnosis was not certain. This had been the object of discussion among my cousins and me for some time. How old was Grandma when she had her mastectomy?

My mother used to talk about visiting her in the hospital and being presented with a new doll—my grandmother having the maternal forethought to have made this purchase before going into the hospital to have her breast removed.

My mother, Ruth, was born in 1920, the youngest of three girls. We figured if my mother were still playing with dolls, the time of my grandmother's mastectomy would have been a little later during that decade. My grandmother, Celia, would have been in her early forties. Although my grandmother survived almost thirty years beyond her mastectomy, diagnosis of breast cancer in a pre-menopausal woman can be a connecting corollary to genetic breast cancer.

I remember seeing my grandmother without her "prosthesis"— a cotton bra stuffed with rags—when I was very young and we lived as an extended family in a three-bedroom apartment in the Bronx: my grandparents, my parents, my unmarried Aunt Anna, and soon my baby brother. My grandmother's chest was horribly deformed, scooped out, almost hollow. And there was a portion of her upper arm, also gone. In those days the word *cancer* was never spoken aloud. The glimpses I saw of my grandmother's scarred chest were an accidental happenstance of all of us living together in an apartment with only one bathroom.

"Why not call to set up an appointment with the genetics clinic?" Dr. P. said. "You have a daughter?" he added.

"And a granddaughter," I told him. Ruthie had just turned six. When Gabi was pregnant, I told her: "If you have a daughter and name her after Grandma Ruth, it will make me happy for the rest of my life." No pressure.

And so. The genetic heritage of personal style. Ruthie has my mother's extroverted flair and confidence. When Ruthie stayed with us in Iowa for a month two summers ago, I enrolled her in a nursery school, and offered to stay for a while the first day thinking she would be nervous, not knowing any of the other children. "No, Grandma," she assured me. "I enjoy meeting new people." Ruthie. Ruth. I love that she is named after her high-spirited great grandmother.

The BRCA gene—what if I tested positive? And what about Gabi? And Ruthie. My cousins didn't have the gene. Yet one of them had cancer. I didn't have cancer, but what if I had the gene? The syndrome that affected my son was genetic in nature, caused by a recessive gene that both my first husband and I carried. Now, happily remarried to a man who is as gentle and steady as my first husband was volatile, I was looking forward to retirement, visiting my grandchildren, some travel. It seemed impossibly bad luck for me to have yet another devastating genetic marker.

"It's a simple blood test," Doctor P. said. He handed me a card: Mary Ellen Carano, RN, MSW: Coordinator of Cancer Resource Center.

On the way out of the clinic, Joe and I passed an ancient couple navigating their way to the elevator. He steered a walker; she had one hand under his elbow, either guiding him or perhaps for her own support. My husband and I were much closer to where they are in this life than any of the families who lined the chairs in the pediatric section we walked by. We kiss goodbye, sometimes before leaving a room. Every day we acknowledge our gratitude for each other. I want time.

My Papa Louis and Grandma Celia, 1912

3

The information from Myriad Laboratories explains: Although the exact risk of breast and ovarian cancer conferred by this specific mutation has not been determined, studies in high-risk families indicate that deleterious mutations in BRCA1 may confer as much as an 87% risk of breast cancer and a 44% risk of ovarian cancer by age 70 in women. Each first degree relative of this individual has a one-in-two chance of having this mutation. If this individual is of Ashkenazi Jewish ancestry, it is recommended that follow-up testing of relatives of this individual include analysis for the mutations 187delAG, 53858hsC.

My students here in Iowa ask: Where are you from? They hear the nasal twang of the borough of my birth. My accent, instead of dissipating after decades in the Midwest, has endured. "The borough of her birth came down through her nasal passages." I think it was Philip Roth who said that. Maybe it was Woody Allen.

I was born in the Amalgamated, named for the Amalgamated Workers Union—a housing cooperative in the Bronx built in the early part of the last century. The Amalgamated was a working class enclave of immigrant Jews where there was a sense of neighborhood as family, a safe place. My mother grew up in the Amalgamated, and the stories she told me of her childhood became as real to me as my own. Of playing Jacks on the roof of the apartment house. Of getting up on a schoolroom desk in P.S. 80 one beautiful autumn day, singing the Depression song: *I Haven't Got a Nickel, I Haven't Got a Dime*—and being expelled for it. She remembered riding home from school on a bus and seeing piles of furniture, pots and pans, clothing, out in the street. Another family couldn't pay the rent and was being evicted.

Her father, my Papa, always had work as a housepainter, though it was hard to picture my mild grandfather on scaffolds higher than anything he could imagine in his village in Eastern Europe. He came to this country without a dollar in his pocket and *"not von vord"* of English.

Grandma came to America by herself when she was just a girl at the beginning of the last century. President McKinley had just been assassinated. The miracle of New York City's subway was still being constructed. My grandmother joined the first exodus of European Jewry, not to seek her fortune or escape religious oppression but to avoid a *shidach*, the arranged marriage her mother had begun. The intended was a man from a distant village, a butcher nearly twice her age. It was all very *Fiddler on the Roof*.

Her intended was older, but it was not so much age that bothered my grandmother. It was height. The groom was apparently short. My grandmother, ever feisty, and probably the most difficult of teenagers, had made "an arrangement" of her own, a plan to get a look before the engagement. She arranged for him to be in the square, under the town clock. The story she used to tell, sitting around the kitchen table in the Bronx: "I took one look at him and told my mother: '*You* marry him. I am going to America!'"

My grandfather was tall. Penniless and illiterate when she knew him as a nice boy from her village—but tall. My grandmother came a few years before he did and sponsored him, lying, and listing him as a brother. Papa was an illegal immigrant. He was also a good man, a quiet, hard worker who never, ever complained. A few years before the Depression, through years of "sweat gelt," he had saved enough to buy his family a modest four family apartment house in the Bronx. But eventually, his out-of-work tenants could not pay the rent. My tough grandmother had the better business sense; she wanted to give the families notice, make them move, and get tenants who could pay. "But how can I throw a family out into the street?" Papa asked. Soon the bank took over and my grandparents themselves were thrown out of the house my grandfather had saved for.

In 1946, soon after my father came home, I was born. There was a housing shortage after World War II, and it was common for generations to live together under one roof. Our apartment was a third-floor walkup, big, with a sunny view of the courtyard. My father went to work with his father in the family fur business on Manhattan's West 29th Street, and my mother stayed home with me. She met her friends with their babies on benches in Van Cordlandt Park. She shopped and took me out for walks. My grandmother did the cooking. Papa sat with me and rubbed my back until I fell asleep.

The first few years of my life were spent in that apartment with my parents, my maternal grandparents and my Aunt Anna, who worked as a secretary at Random House Publishers in the City. In the morning I would go into my aunt's room and watch as she dressed, enamored of her nylons, the perfume, the jangles of costume jewelry. "Now which pin do you think I should wear?" she'd ask me. "Which scarf goes better with this dress?"

For the first three years of my life (before my brother was born) there were five adults in the apartment and me. Five adults who listened to me, sang to me, kissed me until my cheeks were numb, carried me from room to room. I was always in somebody's arms. It is a wonder I ever learned to walk.

We got the call from the genetics clinic that the results were in from the blood test; again, my husband said he would go with me. It was a Friday. This time I didn't tell him not to. Unwelcome medical news should not be received on a Friday. Or alone.

My second husband's name is Joe. Same as my ex. This caused great confusion for while. On our first date together some mutual friends walked into the restaurant. "Fern!" David called out; he seemed delighted: I was dressed up and not as bereft as he had last seen me, although I was still freshly divorced. Then, realizing who was sitting across the table from me, David added, "And Joe! Joe Geha!" David called to his wife who had been hanging up her coat: "Look who's here: It's Fern and Joe!" He and his wife both looked over their shoulders, smiling, as they walked to their table.

The next day another friend called: "Are you and Joe back together?" she asked, shocked. "I heard you were."

"Not *that* Joe, I told her.

For months after we were dating, I called him by his full name to my family and friends so they would not confuse him with my ex, the first Joe—Joey—whose last name I still shared. "Joe Geha and I went to the movies last night..." I'd begin. "I had Joe Geha over for dinner..." It sounded formal. I continued for a while even after we were married. My second husband said he was the only person he knew who was called by his full name in his own house.

The genetics clinic is part of the Bliss Cancer Center, which is part of the Mary Greeley Hospital serving Ames. One of the best things about living in a small city is how easy it is to get around. Even with our recent "sprawl," the entire city of Ames is only about six miles across at its farthest points. There's never traffic when we come home from a dinner party. Hardly ever a crowd at a movie theater. There are restaurants that take

Leaving Long Island...and other departures

reservations, but these are rarely needed. And the doctors are pretty much in one place, a large clinic just about a mile from downtown.

Surprisingly, I had not obsessed over the test. I had tickets to fly to New York to attend my high school's 45th reunion, and I was looking forward to that. At our only other reunion, the 20th, everyone looked good. The pretty girls were still pretty girls. Some of the boys had salt and pepper hair as if they were powdered unevenly for the high school play. We were not yet forty years old, the age some of our children are now.

Joe was quiet, not uncharacteristically, as we drove to the clinic. Mary Ellen, the genetics counselor at the Bliss Cancer Center, smiled when she welcomed us. I looked closer and tried to read her.

With my family history I believed that cancer would be the cause of my eventual demise. But I put the emphasis on "eventual." My head wasn't in the clouds. Potential cancer. I took it seriously. Sometimes neurotically. Mostly realistically.

Six years earlier I had signed up for an ovarian cancer study in Des Moines. I felt I was doing something important for scientific research. I was also proactively having my own ovarian cancer watch. Every month, I saw the nurse who ran the study. She took blood to check for levels of a chemical called CA 125. Although a positive reading does not conclusively indicate the presence of ovarian cancer, I figured a closely monitored study couldn't hurt. Every few months for six years when I received the news *CA 125 within normal limit,* I breathed a sigh of relief.

To qualify for the study, participants had to be "high risk"— that is, they previously had cancer or had a family history of breast or ovarian cancer. Being an Ashkenazi Jew got you high-risk bonus points. Ashkenazi Jews. We love extra credit!

We have high SAT scores. We're successful. But we have some genetic combinations that should give pause to the notion that we are the chosen people.

Mary Ellen walked with a sense of purpose to fetch the oncologist. She was tall and thin, dressed fashionably with a large belt around her slender waist and a blouse poofing out a bit at the hip—like Katy Keene in the old comics. Joe was sitting next to me holding my hand. "This is Dr. Otteman," Mary Ellen said. I told him that, years ago, I had spoken with him on the phone when my mother came to Iowa to live with us the last months of her life. It was through Dr. Otteman that I had ordered my mother's morphine.

Mary Ellen and Doctor Otteman flanked us on either side; he cleared his throat. Of course. Of course. What was I thinking? Good news could have been delivered on the phone. We wouldn't have to come in to meet with an oncologist. Then: "You did test positive for the BRCA1 gene," Doctor Otteman said somberly.

My reaction was immediate, before he had even finished describing the genetic mutation: "What?!!" Followed by an explosion of curses: "Shit! Shit! Fuck. Are you serious? Fuck! Fuck! I can't believe this." There was a reversion—almost primal—to my authentic New York self.

And why was I cursing, angry and almost personally affronted with this news? Where was the surprise, with cancer running up and down my family line like the el train on Jerome Avenue?

Mary Ellen had a packet of information and some brochures on her lap. Following my outburst both she and the doctor were silently sympathetic. Joe patted me, looking stricken. I started crying. Doctor Otteman passed a box of tissues. Although the recent mammogram and ultrasound did not show anything significant, he suggested I have an MRI. Just to make sure.

It is no wonder health care in this country is so expensive. We schedule all these tests. Many agree it seems wasteful to schedule every test under the sun "just to make sure." Unless, of course, it's your own life that you want to "make sure" of. Then bring on the tests. We made an appointment for Monday morning and were assured that the MRI would be read immediately. Joe and I could come back Monday afternoon at 4:00.

So I did indeed have the gene. Specifically: 187delAG BRCA1. **_Deleterious_** was printed in bold.

Dancing with Dad at Barbara's wedding, 1971

4

In 1941, the Nazis burned alive 1,000 Jews in the largest Temple in Bialystok. In the summer of 1943, Himmler issued an order to Gauleiter Erich Kock, the head of the Bialystok general district, and to the local commander of the Security Police to liquidate the Bialystok ghetto.

The final liquidation of the ghetto met with stiff resistance from the Jewish Underground, which fought back, and many Jews found their death inside the ghetto during this uprising. But the Bialystok ghetto, the last ghetto in the entire district, was finally liquidated. The total number of Jews from Bialystok who were deported and murdered in Treblinka came to about 118,000...

(Archives from *Yad Vashem*)

Hitler was an inept scientist. He had exactly the wrong idea about a pure master race, so strong and perfect. Mixing the races (what he referred to as "mongrelization") makes for a stronger stock. Insular communities tending to intermarry only among themselves—like Ashkenazi Jews—reproduce genetic possibilities, the good *and the truly deleterious.*

Jews are not alone in having diseases associated with ethnic heritage. Sickle cell anemia is identified with people of color. The Amish—descended from a Swiss/German gene pool—are being studied for a crippling children's disease not seen in the general population. But while there are more-or-less clearly defined ethnic groups, it's complicated to define what being "Jewish" means. It's a religion. Though not something you can opt out of if you are non-observant. My family was not religious, but my grandparents were certainly Jewish chauvinists. I had been brought up to believe that being smart and telling good stories was more important than being pretty—but lucky I was that, too, my father affirmed. Chosen, indeed.

Once I told a friend that my father often woke me in the morning when I was a little girl by standing in the doorway of my bedroom and calling my name and when I looked up from the pillow, he would say: "*Oy*, you are such a *mieskeit* that I can't even stand to look at you in the morning!" Then he would pretend to call to my mother who was busy in the kitchen making breakfast, to come up and see me, to look at what a *mieskeit* her daughter was in the morning. When I told my friend what *mieskeit* meant—it is Yiddish for ugly face—she was appalled. "*That's* what your father used to call you?" she asked

"Well, he was teasing," I quickly explained. "He didn't mean I really had an ugly face."

She shook her head. "But didn't you feel bad? I think that's so mean, to call a child 'ugly.' To say that you can't stand to look at her."

I was astonished. Telling the story, seeing it through another person's eyes, I guess I could understand how my father's teasing could be interpreted. But why then, in my entire life, did I *always* know, that what my father meant those mornings when I lifted my face from the pillow was: *You are so beautiful and I love you so much, that I can hardly bear to look at you.*

My brother did well in school, skipping grades and testing out. He was also a good athlete: icing on the cake. When my brother did not get into any of the Ivy League colleges he applied to in 1967, the guidance counselors were baffled. The reason suggested was that these schools preferred "geographical distribution." This can also be read: *No more smart, Long Island Jews.* What goes around, comes around. Perhaps one of the reasons my daughter got into NYU law school was because she was "from" Iowa. I helped with her personal statement: "I have a Midwestern work ethic..." This made Gabi seem right off the farm.

Papa—who eventually taught himself to read—had books about famous Jews and Jews who *should* have become famous had they received the recognition they deserved from the gentile world of power. My grandfather had theories about who really invented the telephone and discovered America and cured diseases—every one a Jew. It was implied in my family there were certain ways of behaving. Jewish children didn't get bad grades in school or become juvenile delinquents. Jewish women didn't keep sloppy homes. Jewish husbands made a good living, didn't go to bars or hit their wives. People who were not good with money had "goyisher kops." Jews respected bookishness and were clearly unenamored of the American fascination with guns and motorcycles.

I'm glad my grandparents weren't alive to have read about Bernie Madoff. They had racial pride, but also shame. *Es a Yid?* That was the first question they'd ask about anyone in the news. A philanthropist, a violin virtuoso, a Nobel prize winner, the occasional baseball player: *Es a Yid?* Their chests would swell with pride. But an embezzling *momza* like Madoff? A whoremonger like Elliot Spitzer: A *shanda*, a shame for all Jews. Anthony Weiner. Don't even say the name.

There's a photograph on the bookcase next to the fireplace in my living room in Iowa. A picture of my maternal Grandmother's family, taken sometime in pre-war Bialystok, Poland. There are my great-grandparents, Fayge (whom I am named for) and Leibel Kapalusnik—the name was changed to Kaplan when my grandmother Celia came to this country. Also in the picture are their two grown daughters. My grandmother Celia is not in the picture, having already come to America. Nor is the youngest child, Morris, whom Grandmother brought over when he was still a young man.

It was the style of portraits in those times to face the camera in dignified severity. No one is touching, although my great-grandparents, both seated, have their hands resting on a shared table.

Bialystok in the late 1800's was a thriving city and by the first few decades of the next century, my great-grandmother had a good business, a grocery store which also sold oats for the horses, the means of transportation at the time. My great-grandmother ran the business because her husband, Leibel, was what was called a *Yeshiva bocha,* spending his time in the synagogue. Perhaps they had made this formal photographic portrait as a gift to their daughter in America and sent it to her: *See how well we are doing here, daughter Celia? We are not as poor as when you left us.* The sisters have jewelry. Their high-necked dresses have embroidery, fancy bibs. My great-grandfather in a bushy white beard, wears the cap that signifies that he is an observant Jew, a scholar, not a working man.

But in 1932, my grandmother Celia returned to Bialystok to see the family she had left so many years before. It was also a vacation of sorts for my Aunt Anna. A long ocean voyage. Anna was barely twenty-one, but her mental health was already quite fragile. She had the first in a series of breakdowns when she attempted to look for work in New York. So her mother decided to take her away for a rest.

It was probably not the most rejuvenating to the spirits of a young Jewish girl, however, to visit Eastern Europe in the 1930's. My grandmother and Aunt sailed on the S.S. Hamburg, a German boat, and although they were treated well on the ship, my Aunt later reported back to the family that the Jews in Europe were afraid. Even more than during the pogroms my grandfather used to talk about, where Jews were taunted and beaten by local thugs, murdered, their houses burned to the ground. Every day there was news of more repression, more restrictions by the government. In America there was still anti-Semitism; even in New York City, my blond, blue-eyed Aunt Anna passed as Christian to get a job. But it was nothing like Europe. The difference to them was very clear.

My grandmother suggested to the family still in the old country that they, too, come to America. Times were hard, but her husband, Louis, my Papa, had steady work as a house painter. She would help them settle in. Papa could get work for the men, as he had for her little brother, Morris.

Perhaps it was difficult to get out of Eastern Europe by then. And perhaps not worth the effort if your business was good, if your own family was growing and settled and you had made Bialystok your home. My grandmother's sister Raisel (whom my brother Raymond is named after) had married a carpenter and she had five young children. There were too many people to start a new life in America. Fayge and Leibel were already old. Bialystok was filled with Jews. What could happen to them all?

When I visited the Holocaust museum in Washington D.C., I was struck by one wall of photographs: survivors holding out their arms, photographed from fingertips to elbows. Just arms. No faces. Each had a number tattooed along the forearm. The arms are elderly. The skin is not taut. I noticed the *hands* of the women. Fresh polish on their nails. Diamond wedding bands on their ring fingers; gold bracelets on their wrists. Horrible as the reality is—the prison numbers etched indelibly on human

My Great-Grandparents Fayge and Leibel Kapaloushnik and their daughters, early 1900s

Aunt Anna and Grandma on *The Hamburg*, 1932

skin—the wall of photographs seemed to me less a record of evil, more an affirmation of spirit. As if to the Nazis: *And even with what you did to me, here I am still. I am bejeweled. I got myself a manicure.*

A different display took my breath away. More photographs. Family pictures arranged in a way so that when you enter the narrow corridor you see at once—down and up, up and down—three levels of family portraits in an illuminated space that ultimately becomes a shrine.

Only family pictures, that's all there is. Mothers and daughters and patriarchs standing tall. Smiling babies and shy toddlers. Awkward teenage girls, Anne Frank look-alikes. Boys in short pants and handsome young men with mischievous grins, just looking for trouble. Scholars in wire-rimmed glasses. Fat, old grandmas with bosoms like pillows. And as a Jew, you realize that any one of those could have been a photograph of your family. The lucky ones escaped to make a new life. And that is why you are here today in this museum.

When my cousins and I were little and asked what happened to the family we saw pictured in our albums, the subject was dismissed. They died during the war, we were told. No details because my mother and her sisters said they didn't know details. But it was because of the Holocaust, I think, that the family turned away from being observant Jews. "How could there be a God and allow that babies in their mother's arms be put in gas ovens?" I remember my grandfather saying: *Hitler.* He could pronounce the name and spit at the same time.

I look at the picture in my living room in Iowa, generations of the family I have never met, burned together in a house of worship in Bialystok or an oven in Treblinka. I look at the photograph now and examine it for clues. What is there in the picture of these dark and somber faces? My Aunt Anna's manic-depression? The fatal gene that caused my son to have a tragic disease? A mutation resulting in a family epidemic of cancer?

5

Night Crazies. Symptoms appear like fireflies setting off the dark. All our defenses are down late at night. Your child, the inner one, is the last to let go before sleep, the first to wake from a dreamy-dream. "Wake me if you can't sleep," Joe says. "I'll keep you company."

Waiting for Monday and the MRI was the longest weekend. There is a website called FORCE—Facing Our Risk of Cancer Empowered. The website was started by a woman named Sue Friedman and it is specifically for women who have genetically linked breast and ovarian cancers or who have the genes for these without a cancer diagnosis. Previvors, we are called. All weekend I was on the website. The reading is both comprehensive and horrifying. There is so much information. There are up-to-the-minute medical articles and message boards with thousands of threads about medical procedures like oophorectomies and breast reconstructions and nipple tattoos; there are personal stories from women desiring babies and grieving for lost libidos and dying sisters; there is advice about dealing with insurance companies and about ways to share the news with family members; there are fashion tips about camisole tops and bathing suits and recommendations for the best doctors. The website is immensely helpful for all the decisions BRCA positive women must make and there is kind of a "you go, girl" tone to the posts. Each choice is personal; the idea is to be supportive. I am awed by the medical expertise of these women. I want to have as much information as I can. But knowing so much also scares me silly.

    I had asked Dr. Otteman for something for anxiety before the MRI, knowing I had to stay very still in the machine and fearing claustrophobia. In fact, I was not put into a tunnel, but had to lie face down on a table that had holes for my breasts. It reminded me of those cardboard backdrops where you take a picture from the wild-west with a cut-out surrounding your head.

Later that morning, Joe drove me home, and after the Ativan wore off, I passed the time cleaning the top of the refrigerator and scrubbing stubborn stains from the hall carpet. "You're bustling," he observed, doing a crossword at the kitchen table. He is languid and slow—the original guy in an easy chair; it unnerves him when I move around quickly through the house. Next I threw out the expired spices in the pantry and washed the bath mats. Dealing with crisis, I go into high gear.

By the time Joe and I went back to the hospital in the afternoon to hear the results, we had figured out that the walk was shorter to the Bliss cancer center if we parked in the back, rather than the hospital ramp. We knew which colored lines to follow along to the elevator. Veterans.

We sat in the same chairs we were in on Friday; I felt as if I had been involved with this genetic research for a month rather than a weekend. I also felt scared. Joe gave me a supportive smile. A squeeze. Again, here we go...

"The MRI shows no sign of cancer now," Dr. Otteman said. I wished I had paid closer attention to the follow up, but the truth was, I was still spinning from the news that I actually had the BRCA gene.

"No cancer now," I repeated. "Now" was the operative word. I had tested positive for the gene. But there was no sign of cancer. So why, when I was over sixty years old and I had this gene, could I have dodged the bullet for all this time? Statistics were tricky. Someone was in that smallest percent to escape the surest probability. That someone could be me.

Doctor Otteman was straightforward; clearly he had given this speech before. There were three options. In the following weeks, I would continue to go over the details again and again: the pluses and minuses, the trade-offs, the dangers, the solaces. There was a buffet of choices. To my mind, all of them bad.

#1 Surveilance: a kind of watchful waiting, with continued mammograms, MRIs, transvaginal ultrasound and testing for CA-125 to screen for ovarian cancer.

#2 Chemoprevention: drugs like tamoxifen, other newer and less tested cancer preventatives.

#3 Preventative surgery: removal of the ovaries and fallopian tubes, prophylactic bilateral mastectomy (removal of the now-healthy breasts).

I sensed the way Doctor Otteman presented choices 1 and 2 that these were on the table only because they were, in fact, real options. But from a medical standpoint: found wanting. I asked the question, THE question, that doctors must be asked time and time again. "What would you recommend if I were your wife?" You can fill in anyone here depending on the disease and the appropriate relationship: *What would you do if this were your child? What would you recommend if I were your mother? What would you say if I were your wife?* Perhaps the good doctor was in a bitter divorce with a woman who was trying to take him for every dime he has ever made. True to the stereotype that Ashkenazi Jews are funny, I could not help but make the cheap joke: "That is, presuming that you like your wife and want to keep her around."

Doctor Otteman smiled slightly. I had to trust his marriage was intact. I needed to trust that although I was in Ames, Iowa and not New York, the doctors here were smart and caring and give good advice. "I would recommend the surgeries," Doctor Otteman said.

That night, I couldn't sleep. My left breast hurt. So before I turned over and changed my position, I thought: Cancer. Even though the MRI was clear. Even though breast cancer was not supposed to hurt. Maybe it was all the squeezing. For the past few days, my hand automatically found my left breast—in the shower, while I was sitting at the computer searching the Internet to read about prophylactic bilateral mastectomies. PBM.

What was the first symptom? I always ask. Numbness in her right hand? A lump in his throat? All the portents of disability and disaster. The good news: *Woke up blind in one eye. We thought it was a brain tumor, turned out to be only a migraine.* Sometimes I have trouble sleeping. Thoughts spin out of control in the middle of the night. Wires hiss in the walls, ready to start the house afire. The yard creaks with broken twigs under the foot of a midnight stalker. Mortality shows up like a bad penny at two, three in the morning. "Do you think these thoughts?" I ask my calm, unruffled husband.

"When I get up in the night to pee," he tells me. "I sometimes think of how many years I have left."

Night crazies are selfish. They extend to my own health and welfare and the people I love. Horrifying as the news of the day is (terrorism, famine, nuclear war), I never worry beyond myself and immediate family.

Sometimes when I can't sleep, I do a complicated math that involves dividing up lottery winnings among family and friends. This is odd since I have never bought a single lottery ticket. Nonetheless, the division gets me to sleep: I have 500,000 dollars to give out to fifty people, and they have to spend it in five days. Something like that. If the winnings are very large, I set up charitable trusts.

Once I confessed this creative counting of sheep to a friend. He thought that was sweet. His own method to get to sleep was to fill up what he called "the magic plane." To fight insomnia, he lies in bed, boarding all the people he doesn't like—"anyone who gives me a pain in the ass"—into the magic plane. After it's filled, the plane flies off into the sunset and he never has to see any one of those people again.

"Does the plane actually crash and kill everyone?" I asked. "Or do they simply just disappear?"

"Hey, whatever you want," he replied. "It's your fantasy."

Joe and I were both up at two o'clock in the morning. He got up to urinate, which at his age he does with some regularity. When he came back to bed I greeted him, wide awake. "As long as you're up...would you take a look at this?" he asked turning on the light. He pulled up the back of his tee shirt. I took my reading glasses from the bedside table. "What do you want me to look at?" And then I saw it: a mole, a faded brown with a variegation; a little rough around the slightly irregular edge.

"No, don't even go there," I warned as he walked across our bedroom to the desk. I had already checked the FORCE website before bed and looked at photos of breasts reconstructed with belly fat. (In every home, the Internet should automatically disconnect past midnight to deny access to pornography enthusiasts and hypochondriacs.)

"Honey, I'll call the doctor in the morning," I assured him. I make the appointments when we want to see a professional with some immediacy. This would be my husband Joe calling with a bleeding head injury: *Oh, next month? Next month is good.* He has no skill in conveying the urgency of symptoms.

But now Joe looked grim and my nose was somewhat out of joint that he was usurping my role as the panicked insomniac whose body is housing a dastardly gene set to go off like a ticking bomb.

I had to teach the next day, but not until the afternoon. We both couldn't sleep. Joe went to the kitchen to get us a glass of ice water to share. Though this would result in further trips to the bathroom. "Do you want to watch some television?" he asked. Often, when he can't sleep, he goes quietly to the tv room, happy with the remote in his hand and no one to stop him as he flips quickly through all the stations. (Seinfeld observation: *men don't just want to know what's on. They want to know what* else *is on.*) One morning Joe told me of an interesting show he saw on the Discovery channel. He had stayed up until dawn watching a team of veterinarians remove a fatty tumor from the neck of a duck.

"No, let's read," I said. There was a novel on my night table. Some of the description was beautifully written, so I started to read aloud. I am a compulsive good-writing sharer. "One more paragraph," I promised after Joe threatened to watch television if I continued.

Leaving Long Island...and other departures

After a while, we turned off the light. I had recently told Joe about a friend who met a man on one of the Internet dating sites. I couldn't remember what she said in her clever ad. "Is she the type of person who likes to walk on the beach and dine in fine restaurants?" Joe asked.

I said: "Try to imagine an ad nobody would ever answer. *Loner with gun collection wants to meet marriage-minded woman.*"

He responded: *Single man—wants to meet comforting woman who will stop these voices in his head.*

My turn: *Lonely mother of five wants healthy man to help with yard work and house payments.*

We went on like this for a while. Talk before sleep.

In the morning, right after the clinic opened, I called dermatology and explained our emergency. I said we were soon going out of town and very concerned. The first part was not true. I described the growth on Joe's back and say the word aloud: melanoma.

Joe had ground the beans for coffee and stood in front of the coffee pot, watching it drip. He looked at me admiringly. What a woman—to get him into a doctor's office with such alacrity.

Before noon, we were in the dermatologist's examination room. Now I was the one sitting in the plastic chair, Joe shirtless and awkward on the table. He is thick-bodied and covered with body-hair; it used to be jet black. Now the hair is tightly curled and grey—he calls himself a silverback gorilla. I nag him about over-eating. He enjoys cooking, but also loves to eat. Just monitor yourself, I say. I am a loving nag. He is always good-natured about this. I warn him: *I am not pushing the wheelchair if you are over two hundred pounds.* Which he already is. Joe stopped smoking when he was in his forties and has been trying to lose the same twenty pounds ever since. In the summer, he walks about the house in a sleeveless white undershirt, his slippers flapping. He stares into the refrigerator, takes out leftover pasta and eats it cold, standing up at the counter. Tony Soprano, without the killer instinct.

The dermatologist, a woman with the smooth, creamy skin of a wedge of brie took a brief look. "Oh, that's benign," she said without a hint of hesitation, going on to explain what a *seracacious caratoma* is—basically an age spot. She handed us a brochure with colored photographs of growths that looked even more disgusting than the one that Joe has on his back. She assured us we were right in coming in to see her, that these can sometimes look like something serious. "That's what I'm here for," she said crisply.

Relieved, we went out for lunch to celebrate. There was a sports bar right by the dermatologist's office, crowded with people at the bar watching a game. Joe and I sat by a large picture window. I ordered a broiled chicken half sandwich with salad and kept my mouth shut when Joe chose fries as the side with his hamburger. Usually I at least raise an eyebrow.

"Benign," he said, enthusiastically biting into his burger. "That must be one of the most beautiful words in the English language."

The trees had all budded, the electric yellow-green that signals the vibrancy of spring. The summer stretched before us now with the knowledge of the decisions I must make. What if Dr. Amin had not thought she felt a lump in my breast? Barbara will want me to come to New York to do the operations. Or at least interview more doctors there. Gabi will want me to come to Chicago. What to do first: Take out my ovaries? Take off my breasts? Do everything at once? If I had it to do over, would I want to know? "I'm so glad I'm with you," I said, reaching across Joe's plate for a french fry.

"Take more," Joe said. "Want a bite of this burger? There's blue cheese and mushrooms. It's great."

My first husband was not a food sharer—not even in a Chinese restaurant. "I ordered just what *I* wanted," he used to say, guarding his dish. Maybe that's reasonable. But his refusal to share made me feel alone.

6

Youthful mid-sixties, good-looking, athletic, university professor, vegetarian nonsmoker. Likes movies, walks on the beach. Good with children and dogs. Excellent bridge player. Ability to use verbal skills as intellectual armor. Wants accommodating woman who is agreeable to mood swings and occasional philandering.

I suppose that's how I'd describe my first husband in a personal ad. I could think of other positive things. Joey was neat. And he could remember jokes. Some people don't like jokes, but I do. Even corny or dirty ones, if the jokes are good ones. So it was fun to be married to someone who remembered jokes and told them pretty well. He was a loving father who changed diapers and made up imaginative games and goodnight stories. I believe my ex would describe me fairly with mention of my generosity and peppy personality. He thought I was smart. But he would also describe my desire to always be right in an argument. And he might mention a vengeful streak.

We had met as teenagers at a party. He was blond and broad-shouldered but he also had sad, soulful eyes. We looked at each other across the floor, then danced in steamy silence to Johnny Mathis singing "The Twelfth of Never." Barbara said, "Fern, I bet you marry him."

"Don't be ridiculous," I said as I started to write his name in all its variations across my world history notebook: Joseph, Joey, Joe.

In the summer of my senior year in high school, he had a job as a lifeguard in a country club in Plainview, Long Island, where I worked as a counselor in the day camp. I remember him up on the stand, caramel-colored, flashing a white smile, the whistle dangling on his muscled chest. A golden boy. That's what my Papa used to call him: Golden Boy. "You Jewish?" Papa would ask. Joey said he was. Then Papa would forget and turn to me. "He's Jewish?" he repeated skeptically.

We married a few weeks before I graduated from college. My friends would soon all be off hitchhiking around Europe before they settled into teaching jobs, but Joey and I had been together so long, that marriage was the inevitable next step. An elopement in May of my senior year, then studying for finals. We would go to Europe together that summer of 1968, but somehow going on this adventure as a married couple didn't seem quite as exciting as going with friends. I didn't tell him that. Married at twenty-one. That age seems so incredibly young now.

I was in love, but I also felt bonded together with him in some ineffable way. High school sweethearts. My whole young romantic life was identified with him. I could never imagine divorce. It would be like divorcing a blood relative.

Although he was handsome and bright, Joey was also quick-tempered and often angry in the least provocative circumstance. I was dependably cheerful. Once he said to a friend of ours that I was "happy on the inside" and he wanted to learn how to be that way. Also he was drawn to my warm and uncomplicated family, because his own was so troubled.

My young husband could be charming and magnanimous, like his mother when she was in good spirits. When he turned moody, however, anger, not silence, was the predominant characteristic. My father told me only after the divorce that he had never liked Joey, never trusted him. "Why didn't you ever tell me?" I asked. Because I had picked him. Because whomever I had chosen, my father would have taken in as family. My mother said, when I told her that we would marry: "Well, you know, Fernie, that I am very fond of him, but he *is* a little crazy."

Maybe a little crazy was what attracted me. Joey had a wild streak that manifested itself in driving too fast, playing too hard and "not taking any shit" from anyone he considered rude or stupid. This included a lot of people. My cousin theorized that he was the closest a good Jewish girl like me could get to a "bad boy."

I planned to teach for a few years, waiting for Joey to finish his graduate degree. I had not given serious thought to "being" something other than a supportive wage-earner, a wife, a mother. It was before feminism had encouraged me to ask questions about what I wanted to do with my own life. I recall a woman at a dinner party confronting me after I had told her Joey and I were going to Iowa after he had finished graduate school. "Well, why would you go to Iowa?" she asked. I was puzzled: Hadn't I just told her of his job offer? I had just spent the past few years with an assorted series of part-time teaching jobs, but I didn't have a resume, much less designs on a career.

"Women always follow men..." she began, making it clear that her career was important to her. "But what are *you* going to do in Iowa?"

It was the first time that I had heard this side of things. That actually, *I* should have had some life goal aside from being my husband's sidekick on our Midwestern journey. "But this is what *I* want, too," I said. And it was.

Later, I recalled all the graduate school couples that my husband and I had been friends with, all of them divorced by their early thirties. Not us, my husband and I would say. "Oh, I'm so glad I'm married to you," he would tell me when we'd come home from a party with graduate student wives, whose newly emerging feminism made the women seem humorless and dowdy.

The summer of 1971 Joey and I drove across the country in a battered Datsun without air conditioning to Iowa where he was to begin his teaching career. Joey insisted that we take all the house plants from our graduate apartment; with the car windows open, the loose dirt blew around from the back seat. The most west I had ever been was Rochester, New York. I thought when we arrived in Ohio: Well, this wasn't such a bad trip! Ohio. Iowa. Idaho. It seemed like one generic plain.

I loved Iowa right away. The gently, rolling fields; the big, blue sky; the basic decency of its people. Every four years when big city journalists swarm the state during the Iowa political caucus, they write articles about how "nice" Iowans are, a description that may seem patronizing; but I've lived here now far longer than I've lived on the East Coast and this observation is basically true.

Though today no one should romanticize life in small-town Iowa. My friends who are Iowa natives say it's changed. Agribusiness conglomerates have taken over many family farms and hurt small-town economies. There's trouble with drugs, methamphetamine in particular. College graduates move, so there's been both a population and brain drain. Still, even today, drive along the county roads and it seems as if you're in a Grant Wood painting. I'm glad that the cities like Des Moines are thriving. Iowa is a great place to raise a family. Leave and then come back, should be our state motto.

In Iowa that first summer Joey and I rented a furnished apartment, fifty-five dollars a month, because we planned on putting a down payment on a house as soon as we could with money my father had given us for a wedding gift. The apartment was a finished basement in the back of an old house. There was plastic furniture, much of it broken, and a refrigerator and shower covered with mold. Before we even unpacked, we purchased brooms and bleach and flowered contact paper to line the kitchen shelves. The first night I saw a centipede the size of my thumb scurry under the stained mattress in the damp, back bedroom.

Joey and I slept on the vinyl couch, one of those where the back folds down, so there isn't quite enough room for two and the sheets always slid off in the middle of the night. In the morning, we woke up sweaty, our bare legs stuck to the plastic. I wouldn't sleep on the bedroom mattress, even when Joey suggested bringing it out into the living room. At least bedbugs couldn't get through vinyl.

We had a routine: Joey taught morning summer school; I shopped and cooked casseroles and circled the ads for houses we'd see later that afternoon. We had no television and no telephone and knew no one else in town. We read and took naps and made love. What else was there to do?

The restaurants were terrible. All served baked potatoes in foil. Iceberg lettuce with orange French dressing. Jello salads. There was no Chinese food. Nothing ethnic. The bakery on Main Street sold doughy white bread and glazed donuts. No bagels. And what passed for pizza forty years ago in central Iowa....

We went on picnics to Hickory Grove and swam in a small lake; when the wind shifted, we could smell the manure from neighboring farms. The sky was so wide, clear and blue. Everyone looked healthy and blond. We took drives out into the country through the endless fields of corn and soybeans. Big lazy cows hung around the periphery of the horizon. We looked at each other, strangers in a strange land. The weather was certainly something to talk about. Our first week in Iowa there were tornado sightings and the sirens warned us to take cover. Since the apartment was already *in* the basement we got into the windowless bathroom and waited. Tornadoes! We actually lived in Iowa.

The house we bought was an old Dutch Colonial with a screened front porch; it was on a street with big trees and older houses, only a few blocks from campus where Joey would be teaching philosophy. We looked at furniture. We had a few thousand dollars saved. It seemed like an enormous amount of money then. Especially when we still had graduate student decorating standards: bricks and boards for book cases; a mattress with an Indian print throw for the living room.

By the end of summer I was pregnant with our first child (conceived on that vinyl couch); Joey had a first job; we had a first house. I made curtains and painted the bedroom yellow. In September, the older faculty members invited us to dinner parties and welcomed us warmly.

Joey and I were fit and tanned from our afternoons swimming at the lake, me plumping up and glowing at the beginning of pregnancy; we must have made an attractive couple. I remember that there was something in the way the older faculty gazed upon us. What did that look reveal if not the sweet pang of memory and desire? I didn't entirely understand the look at the time. I do now, though.

That first summer in Iowa was one of the happiest times of our marriage. It was an adventure. Coming to a place where we knew no one. Still in our twenties, but playing grown-up, going out with real estate agents to look at real houses. It was *just us*. And I think we both felt a little proud at how well we were making it, getting along all by ourselves with no family or friends.

The "just us" of our situation that summer had a resonant echo from my husband's life. Joey was the only child of an unhappy marriage. His father told jokes but kept secrets and never seemed to make a good enough living to suit his wife who, despite her own working class roots, had grandiose airs. "Queen Muriel," we called her. A Hunter College graduate, but bitter because she was a secretary for male bosses never near as smart as she.

She was also a beauty with a highly dramatic style. I was amazed the very first time I saw her when Joey brought me to his parents' apartment on Cherry Ave in Flushing. Tall and elegant, Muriel was at the stove, actually stirring a chocolate pudding. She was wearing a figure-hugging, gold outfit—I think the material was called Banlon—a turtleneck and matching stirrup, stretch pants. She had half a dozen gold, bangle bracelets up her arm; her dark hair was pulled severely back in a bun at the top of her head, not a librarian-type bun, but a prima ballerina-type bun; she wore false eye-lashes (I had seen false eyelashes on movie stars, not on someone making pudding); and in her left hand—the one without the wooden spoon—dangled a long, cigarette holder which secured a Pall Mall, unfiltered. "Hello, dear," she said in a sultry alto and took a deep drag. Smoke swirled above her head. She looked like the Dragon Lady from Terry and the Pirates.

I was in jean cut-offs and sandals; my hair was in a perky flip. I was sixteen and weighed 101 pounds, but immediately felt even younger and smaller. "Hi," I said, but what ran through my mind was: *Boy, I'm glad she's not* my *mother.*

Muriel was a difficult woman, prone to migraines and dark moods, later an alcoholic in full force. Occasionally, following some offense when she didn't feel appreciated, she didn't speak to husband or son for days, even weeks, at a time.

When Joey was ten years old, the family went on a vacation to a lakeside cabin. "It's *just us*," his mother kept repeating on the drive up. "So it's up to us to make our own good time." What was unsaid must have weighed on Joey and his father, for they worked hard to see the rustic beauty in what turned out to be a run-down summer cabin on a remote lake.

What happened was this: the weather was awful, his parents fought, his mother sulked and withdrew. Father and son went out in a fishing boat while Muriel took to her bed in the cabin, not talking to either of them. "It's just us," Joey recalled his father repeating, as they fished in the rain. "It's just us." His joking-around father must have meant the phrase ironically, but recalling this event years later, the truth of the observation made Joey profoundly sad.

Eventually, Joey's father had an affair; divorced Muriel after a twenty year marriage; married someone much younger, a dull woman, but anxious to please. Very soon after the divorce, his father and second wife had a baby girl.

During the tumultuous year following his parents' divorce, Joey had a blow-out fight with his father and new wife. Joey threw furniture from their new dining room set, breaking the legs of a chair, and stormed out of their apartment. He was twenty-one years old and his new baby half-sister was sleeping in her crib.

For years after we moved to Iowa, Joey did not see or call his father. I kept encouraging him, especially after our own daughter was born, to get back in touch. One late night after a couple of beers, Joey finally called. "I'm sorry," he said, when he heard his father's sleepy voice. The apology was for waking everyone up. It was after midnight on the East Coast.

No, no, his father insisted, so happy to hear from him. They didn't stay on the phone for that long, but made promises to see each other when we returned that summer for a visit to Long Island. "Everything's all right," his father said, dismissing the years of silence. And also perhaps the betrayal and deceit to their first family. So it was with an almost eerie preordination that a few weeks before our twentieth wedding anniversary, I discovered that Joey, the son, repeated almost the exact script of his father's life.

Fern, Joey and his mother, Muriel, 1968

7

When I was in counseling, the therapist confronted me: You're a smart woman. Didn't you know what was going on?" I told her that I didn't and, at the time, it was the truth. In retrospect, I believe I did know. Not in any conscious part of me. If someone had asked me: Is your husband seeing another woman? I would have said no. I believed it, too.

But in fact, he had been unfaithful before. I used to look at couples who did their grocery shopping together or went on walks after dinner. Not us. Sometimes I'd think that it was good that we were independent and gave each other space. We had many of our own friends and interests. Joey went to the gym every day, worked out and went running a few times a week with a woman who had been his student. She even came to the gym pool we had rented where Gabi had a swim birthday party for her ninth birthday. The pool was filled with squealing little girls; Joey organized the games of water basketball and Marco Polo before he left for a run with Debbie. She was short, dark and unhappy looking. She had told him about her problems with men; he liked to be the confidante, the wise mentor. He was helping her. And he shared this with me. Why would I be jealous?

But a few weeks after Gabi's birthday party, I saw them driving in her car together and suddenly I knew. He denied it when I asked if there was something more to this relationship. He said that I was crazy, how could I think that? Then I did something that was actually crazy. I went to Debbie's apartment. I saw her in the window of her first floor duplex, but when she saw me, she quickly left the room. I banged and banged on the door, yelling for her to open. It was the middle of the day, and there were people walking along the street. I picked up a rock and threatened to smash in the window if she didn't let me in.

Debbie looked small and scared to death when she finally opened the door, her dark eyes darting around the room. "Do you want to hit me?" she asked. Why was she afraid? She was the one who worked out all the time, not me. I told her she could have him if she wanted. I don't know why I said that. She shook her head. "He really loves you," she said. "Not me." It was like a country and western song.

That night he cried. "I don't know why I did this," he said. He told me he loved me. He made me promise not to tell anyone and pleaded with me to forgive him. I said I would. But sometime after he seemed hostile rather than chastened. I thought he was angry at getting caught. We put the ugliness in a deep place away from our ordinary family life. So eight years later, I was surprised. Though I shouldn't have been.

I ran into Joey on campus a few weeks after our divorce was final; he said *hi*, then added that he liked my hair. I should have been prepared to see him since we both taught at the university. I still thought of him as my husband, not my ex. Yet I didn't say hello nor did I respond to his compliment about my new haircut. I just looked at him—really, there were no words *in* me to respond at that time. There he was, striding across the lawn on a sunny day, a man I had lived with for almost twenty years, the father of my children, a person whose habits of being, whose sounds and smells were as familiar to me as my own. "I like your hair," he said, giving me a sheepish smile.

Some people feel quite amicable about their exes but I've always found the idea of a friendly and affectionate divorce hard to understand. When we were getting divorced, Joey suggested that perhaps sometime we could go out to dinner together. He hoped that we could always be *friends*.

He had seemed distant for months before our split. I thought he was preoccupied because he was on leave from the university and supposed to be writing a book. Sometimes I saw him looking unhappy, lost in thought. "Is anything wrong?" I'd ask. "No," he'd say, sighing.

I don't know how people in other occupations manage affairs, but really there's no better profession for infidelity than university teaching; except for meeting classes about nine hours a week and going to committee meetings, your time is your own. You can say you were huddled up in a study carrel on the third tier of the library doing research on Asian mollusks and who could be the wiser?

When I was in college at the end of the Sixties, one of my friends was having an affair with a married professor. It was hard for me to see this affair as the romance she envisioned, and our female friendship became sorely strained. I was too judgmental, she said. Disapproving. We were all young and hip and it was the Sixties, after all. Uptight, square, was something you didn't want to be called when you saw yourself as young and free. And wasn't there something thrilling about having an affair with an older, powerful man?

The professor would call our apartment. He used to come over and leave his shoes outside my friend's bedroom door. Professor T had big feet and man-styled shoes, not the workboots or athletic shoes of the boys we dated. He was a very flamboyant storyteller who made himself the hero in every tall tale. He had three children and a stay-at-home wife.

Dr. T was one of those tortured, angry men whose station in life (in this case being an English teacher at a mediocre state college) was a few stops short of where he wanted to be. Dr. T used to call late at night and my friend would drive somewhere remote to meet him, taking a couple of joints and a blanket from her bed in our college apartment. He had a guitar and would play for her. Then they would put down the seats of his Chevrolet Suburban and she would perform oral sex.

One weekend I saw Dr. T sitting with his wife at a concert. The wife was small-boned and pretty, with thick auburn hair. She was laughing with him and I noticed that she had her hand on her husband's leg in a proprietary way.

Even at twenty years old, I identified more with the wife of the professor than I did with my girlfriend who thought she was in love. My husband-to-be was in graduate school planning to be a college professor. Perhaps I saw my own future as The Betrayed Wife looming ominously.

Another part of it, I guess, had less to do with traditional values and more to do with common sense. My girlfriend was seduced by flattery. Dr. T was a bullshit artist and an alcoholic. My friend sat rapt as he went on and on. Dr. T told her how beautiful she was, how inspired he was by her vitality. He wrote poems for her. But no matter how my friend presented this relationship, my idea of romance did not include running out of the house at midnight to give blow jobs in the back of a family station wagon.

It was two weeks before our twentieth anniversary, a Saturday morning in April when I found out. I saw the letter in a girlish script in my husband's desk. I read the words: "Thank you for letting me love you." The black ink looked like snakes to me. Joey confessed that he had been having an affair. He looked stricken. Again, the young woman was a student; she had been in his class the semester before. I'd sat next to her once at a lecture sponsored by the philosophy department. She was blond, in her twenties, with the bland wholesomeness of an egg. But this time he told me, "I don't think I love you anymore."

Within days, I had packed up the extra linens, a set of dishes and was circling the apartments listed in the local paper. It was not that I was so very sure then of my decision to end the marriage. It was also my over-drive-in-crisis reaction. Ironically, getting a divorce at that point still seemed to be *my* decision. I don't think he would have moved out of our house quite so quickly had I not taken action.

He suggested marital counseling, but only with the condition that he could still see his girlfriend. When I explained to him how that was impossible, he tried to reason with me. At one point he said: "Fern, if we go to counseling and it doesn't work out between us, then I will have no one."

So I went to therapy on my own. I recall once using the word "wrong" in describing my husband's behavior and the therapist's eyebrows arched quizzically. "Wrong" isn't a word that is frequently used in therapeutic jargon. *Wrong. Adultery.* It's true the words have a fire-and-brimstone ring. You hear people talk about the extra-marital affairs and they say: *it just happened.* As if having affair doesn't take some preparation. Giving out phone numbers. Arranging a place to meet. There's a lot of time to contemplate what you are doing before an affair actually begins. It's not like falling off a diet when you eat a slice of chocolate cake that someone puts before you.

Perhaps I moved so quickly toward divorce because I was afraid not to. I was not teaching then and was home full-time working as a writer; a chick-lit novel, some advertising brochures that Barbara had sent my way. That year my writing had earned me a little more than fifteen thousand dollars—money that was actually pretty good for a writer—but not something I could live on for the rest of my life. Also, as a divorced person I would have no health insurance. I was forty-two years old and I could still get a teaching job easily enough. And if I didn't have the health insurance—well, at least I had my health.

Serendipitously, I met a woman at an academic conference during this time. We ate lunch together and I've never seen her again—but her presence then served as some sort of omen. She was a smart-looking woman, silver-haired, perhaps in her middle-fifties. A few years before, her husband had left her for a thirty-year old woman hired to build a bed of perennials in their backyard garden. The children were grown and gone. She had been devastated following the split, and shortly after was hospitalized for colitis. She was ok now, she said. Although she was sorry that, in a rage, she had pulled up all of the peonies and day lilies.

I looked at her long and hard across the table. Even given all the history my husband and I had together, did I want to work to continue a marriage with someone who couldn't be trusted?

Sometime soon after, when Joey and I had been having a conversation about counseling, I told him, "No, I want a divorce." I remember how dramatically his tone changed when I said those words. How he went from soft and placating to furious. "Ok. Fine. If that's what you want. You got it!" His face twisted in a menacing snarl. I was used to his mood changes.

How jocular, cajoling, could turn nasty in a matter of seconds. I had frequently thought during the fights we used to have: *How did we end up here?"*

A week before I would have told anyone that I was in an enduring marriage. Suddenly I was getting divorced. But it was Joey's real coldness to me during that time that made me come to grips with the kind of relationship we had had together for so many years. Lights kept going off in my head—pop! pop! pop! Or click! click! click! like those mini epiphanies that used to be printed in Ms. Magazine.

It is one thing to fall in love with someone else, but quite another to then act *yourself* as if you were the injured party. Perhaps he needed to demonize me in order to extricate himself from the relationship. I used to be sweet, but now, in middle age, I was controlling, he told me. I had too many friends; I didn't make him feel special. I was materialistic—I had wanted to remodel our kitchen—while he was inclined to pursue a more spiritual realm.

One time during the separation he came over to the house to get some tools. He and his girlfriend were putting together some bookcases he had in the new apartment. He began telling me what a pleasure it was to work with her on a construction project. He told me admiringly how mechanical she was, a Midwestern farm girl, deft at using the carpenter tools. He shook his head: "You were never handy," he lamented.

I was married for almost twenty years to a difficult man. I saw him that way during our marriage. He hated when I said that—that he was difficult. But it takes two to make the tenuous tango work, to create the dance that you perform together in the world. I was a partner in that dance.

He never did anything he didn't want to do. And I didn't balk. This I remember, and it makes me angry now although I don't recall feeling angry at the time: going to my first natural childbirth class alone. I had signed up for the class a few months before. We had gone to some hospital talks and took a tour of the nursery. In my seventh month of pregnancy I enrolled for the natural childbirth classes that were just starting to be popular. All of my friends had taken them. The evening class started at seven-thirty and I was getting ready one night, gathering the material we were supposed to bring: the pillow, a notebook. I remember Joey in the bedroom watching television—it was a vampire movie that he had wanted to see—and he was lying on the bed, his shoes off. I said that we should get going. And I think I was tentative, apologetic. He hated being told when to go places.

He was annoyed. Said how this was a movie he really wanted to see. This was almost forty years ago, so of course we couldn't tape it. He asked whether we couldn't be a little late. I was already standing there in the doorway with my coat on, the front unbuttoned over my swollen belly. I was twenty-five years old and had a long braid down my back, hippie style. I thought I was independent and free.

It was actually me who suggested that Joey not go with me to the natural childbirth class. I remember feeling that this was an experience that he should *want* and I didn't want to be the one who made him resentful for forcing him to participate. I told him I didn't mind going by myself. That I'd take notes and tell him what went on. Did I actually mind at the time? Probably, I just did not want to go with him grouchy about missing his movie and having to be someplace he didn't really want to be.

I don't think I realized how very odd it would be for me to be in a gymnasium all so neatly coupled. As it turned out there was one other woman who was there by herself who became my partner for the labor exercises. It was 1971. She told me that her husband was in Vietnam. I didn't tell her that my husband was at home watching a vampire movie.

Seventeen years later, the night I had actually found out about his affair, Joey and I stayed up late talking, fighting, crying. But he also seemed agitated, energized by his new love. And closed off from me. He did not want to go round and round. He did not want to answer all the questions I had. Finally he said: *I can't do this anymore.* Annoyed. Within the next few minutes, he turned from me in bed and was soundly sleeping. I wanted to bash his head in.

I went into the study and went right to the computer and started to write. Because that's what I often did when I was trying to make sense of something. Use my words. Talk it out with friends. Write it out. Later, I sold what I wrote that night to a woman's magazine. It was an article called: "I Don't Think I Love You Anymore." It took me less than two hours to write and I sold the article for two thousand dollars. It was the most money, per hour, that I ever made as a writer.

This was in the time before email made it so easy to communicate, but women all around the country, sat down and made the effort to write me letters. Some counseled me to hang in there, to try and save my marriage. Others wrote, devastated, to tell me about their own long-married husbands who had left for secretaries, students, assisting nurses—usually the closest womanly, warm body within reach. Others gave me inspiring pep talks. Life will be good for you, they promised. Just wait and see.

Joey was appalled that I wrote and published the article. He said that writing about our relationship just as it was falling apart was a sure sign of a desire to control my version of the story and inability to respect any sense of privacy. I said that perhaps he shouldn't have fallen asleep when I was in mid-sentence.

Ultimately, he requested that half of the two thousand dollars I received for the article was his due. We were still married at the time that I wrote it. Iowa is a no-fault divorce state, which means that all of your marital resources are divided, no matter who did what to whom. "And if it weren't for me, you never would have written that article," Joey said. One of my friends observed it was like Hitler saying he wanted a part of the royalties from Anne Frank because without him, that Diary would never have been published.

My lawyer—I think out of some chivalrous response to protect me, the woman scorned—took an immediate dislike to my ex. Or maybe it's just because lawyers are always supposed to be on their client's side. My lawyer questioned. Joey responded tersely but was quietly hostile throughout the deposition. My lawyer asked pointedly about the girlfriend: "And do you view your relationship as permanent or not?"

Joey answered, showing off his philosophical acumen: "Well, we'd have to get into a metaphysical discussion on the nature of permanence, wouldn't we?" My lawyer and the soon-to-be ex looked fiercely across the table at each other. Jaws tightened. Rams locking horns.

I read an article written by a family therapist whose own long-term marriage ended in betrayal and who found herself still occasionally "stunned" with anger and suffering even years later, but ultimately saw forgiveness as a kind of transcendence. I admired the sensibility but for years after did not work very hard toward forgiveness. Too easily I could become again one of those women who, at the merest encouragement, could simply rewind the tape: *Do you know what that bastard did to me…? Do you know what that bastard did to me…?* A part of me understands that forgiveness enlarges our spirit; that true forgiveness is not a giving up or giving in, but allows us the most supreme act of generosity and human kindness. Then another part of me concludes: *Ah, fuck him.*

Of course, in a selfish way, real forgiveness also means that we can finally come to see in a clearer light who we were in the relationship with our ex's and who we have become. Forgiveness is about discovering ourselves. "You'll see," Joey assured me as he was walking out the door. "You'll survive. You might even see one day that this might be the best thing that ever happened to you."

Our divorce after a twenty-year marriage stunned everyone who knew us. Including me. A friend said: "I thought if you two survived Zachariah, you could survive anything."

8

On a visit back to Long Island, I ran into a girl I went to high school with. She had just read the book I had written about Zachariah. "I'm so sorry," she said. "You were always such a happy girl." When I told her that I was still happy, the assurance sounded hollow. How could I ever be happy again?

Barbara's daughter has become a terrific photographer. Liza lives out on Long Island in a big, suburban house with a swimming pool, three kids, dogs and a husband who takes the Long Island railroad into the city every morning. Last summer, Liza took about two hundred pictures when our families were together. But there was one that made me gasp: Gabi and her son, Wilson—he was about three then—sitting in a rocking chair—the way his head rests against her shoulder, his light hair in angel curls around his head, his big, blue eyes. He looks sweet and sleepy against his mom, his mouth slightly agape. Like Zachariah. They looked so much alike that it took my breath away.

Barbara had forwarded the picture to me (*Do you believe this!!*) and I forwarded it along to Zachariah's father, my ex, with a friendly email. He is now on wife number three, a very nice, age-appropriate woman who used to be a nurse. So time does heal all wounds. Or at least scabs them over sufficiently. I am glad for him. Also, I recognize that at our age it's good to be with someone who has medical expertise.

My ex and I are not exactly friends as he'd proposed so many years ago, but I am no longer angry, no longer have mutilation fantasies or wish him anything bad at all. He was the father of the children we both loved with all our hearts.

He emailed me back right away: *Thank you so much for the photo of Will. He does look so much like Zachy. I sometimes wonder whether my enthusiasm for him is due to the similarities and the fact that he is such a robust little replacement for our boy.*

How many children do you have? It's hard to answer. One freezing, February night years ago, we had a job candidate visit the English department. I sat next to my second husband at dinner in the best restaurant in Ames. We were trying to woo this man to Iowa State, to impress him with the positive aspects of living in a Midwestern college town with a wind chill factor of minus twenty degrees. The man had small children, so I had been talking about how good the Ames public schools were. I said that our youngest daughter was about to graduate. "Our three girls..." I began. "So you have the three children," he responded.

"Well, Fern had..." Joe began before I gave him a look, a subtle shake of my head. *Don't go there,* the look said.

Around the table, there were people who knew. Others who did not. And there is no way to casually bring up Zachariah at a table where people are drinking wine and passing around appetizer platters of bruschetta and calamari. There is no way to say to a polite inquiring stranger among a group of others: *Oh, I had a son who died at sixteen of a genetic deteriorating brain disease,* without making the person feel terrible for asking in a social setting and then feel terribly sorry for *you.* And of course, *his* stunned sadness is totally new. Your enduring sadness had years and years to develop so you can't exactly get to the place where you seem appropriately sorrowful *with* a stranger.

Zachariah was a baby almost too pretty to be a boy. He had golden curls and long, fringy lashes around the biggest, bluest eyes. We didn't know it right away, but Zachariah would be severely handicapped, suffering from Canavan's disease. This is similar to Tay-Sach's, a better known disease. Canavan's, like Tay-Sach's, has an autosomal-recessive genetic origin. That means that both parents—although not affected themselves—carry this deadly gene. Recent research shows that the gene is carried by one in forty Ashkenazi Jews. It affects both the brain and the central nervous system because there is a deficiency of the enzyme aspartocyclase, necessary for normal brain development. Those affected cannot generate myelin, which insulates nerve cells and permits transmission of nerve impulses. The children appear normal at birth but never develop beyond infancy. Many die before they are five years old and are ultimately immobile, blind and severely retarded. If there is a more cruel future planned for a baby that a woman wanted with all of her being, I do not know of one.

The disease is endemic to Jews of a certain region of Eastern Europe: Vilna, Lithuania. Both my first husband and I could trace our families to this ancestral turf. For me, that would be on my father's side. It was most likely my mother's family that had the BRCA gene for hereditary cancer. But Ashkenazi once again.

Canavan's disease was so rare when Zachariah was born in 1976 that no doctor we first met had even heard of it. Also, living in Iowa, there was no recommended screening for any "Jewish" diseases. The odds of this, for my first husband and me to have this specific gene for a disease that had only been recorded in a few families was very slim. There was no history of this in all the generations we knew of, only going back to our grandparents who had left Eastern Europe. Yet, there we were, blond and blue-eyed in Iowa, betrayed by some tribal memory: the final pogrom.

I "knew" about Zach, though not the name or the extreme nature of the disease, before anyone else—even the pediatrician who intimated that perhaps I was an over-anxious mother—you know those university types who want their kids reading at six months.

Fern and Zachariah, 1979

Gabi and Wilson, 2008

When Gabi was born four years before, I had not been prepared for the gushy-rush of maternal love that I felt when she was placed in my arms. Immediately there was that unseverable bond, that fierce protective surge. During the following days in the hospital, still drug-high and with post-operative pain from the C-section, I'd look into her eyes, so close, then falling asleep together. I was never sure where I left off and she began...flesh of my flesh, bone of my bone.

It had been different with Zach. I didn't exactly know why. Perhaps because he was a second child. Perhaps because he was a boy. But I just didn't feel the same kind of connection, that primitive maternal passion.

In retrospect I don't know that I would have felt differently if Zachariah had been normal. He certainly looked normal enough those first few months to fool us all, to fool the obstetrician who had also delivered Gabi and said what terrific babies her dad and I made.

But unlike his placid sister, Zach was a cranky, unresponsive baby who had great difficulty sucking and could not be soothed. He seemed hungry, but couldn't seem to get enough to eat. He was always constipated. He didn't seem to have enough control over his muscles to make things work right.

I tried putting into words my concern to our pediatrician, but I couldn't explain what seemed to be lacking in Zach. He assured me that irritable crying was normal with many babies. That I had been "lucky" that Gabi had been such an easy infant. I tried to explain my fears to his father after I had seen a baby about Zach's age —four or five months—in the supermarket. The baby had a bright, alert look that seemed to take everything in. Not like Zach who I used to describe as "blurry."

I reread Dr. Spock: *Every baby's face is different from every other's. In the same way, every baby's pattern of development is different from every other's.* I went into Zach's room to see him sleeping peacefully in his crib, his cherubic mouth in a pout. He looked perfect. Why was I worried about him?

We started going for the tests when Zach was about five months old and still could not hold up his head. And the next few years, spent in hospitals and clinics, with therapists and special educators—well, the details could have filled a book. And so I began to write. When students ask how I became a writer, I tell them about Zachariah. Surely one of the most rewarding aspects of my life came from the most painful.

In January 1980, *Redbook* magazine published an article I wrote about Zachariah and the decision his father and I made for residential placement. It was called "A Place for Zachariah." The accompanying photograph, a beautiful family portrait, later used for the cover of the book, took up almost the whole page. The magazine had flown a photographer from New York to take our picture. "Ah," I remember the photographer saying as she snapped away. "Hold it. Hold it. Perfect."

Zach, exhausted from crying, had just begun to fall asleep on his father's shoulder. Zach is in the middle of the shot, dressed in blue, his golden curls forming a halo around his head. Gabi, age seven, leans in on her dad. Her mouth is closed in the photograph, but I recall that her two top teeth were missing then. My right hand is placed across Zach's wrist; I lean in as if for a kiss. Who was I then? It is a photograph of a young mother and her lovely family forever stopped in time.

Zachariah lived with us for the first few years of his life, but I knew that his care would eventually preclude any semblance of a normal life for the rest of us. When there was an opening, we placed him in a home for severely handicapped children in Dubuque, Iowa. The home was started by a woman who had her own child there and it gave me some comfort knowing Zach would be well taken care of. I recall holding Zach that last day and giving him over to the outstretched arms of a nurse at the facility. He was in yellow pajamas and clean from a bath. She cradled him against a large, comforting bosom and made soft, clucking sounds.

Joey loved Zach so. He roughhoused with Zach and played wild-boy wheelchair games; Zach's laugh used to fill the room. In some ways, in the place where fathers and sons toss baseballs around in their heads, my athletic first husband must have longed for the son he might have had—and hurt even more than I.

For a long time, being Zachariah's mom defined me. For many years I made it my mission to speak around the country about the rights of families to have safe places for the most profoundly needy of our children. The politics were often against me. The home. The home was the best place for any child, the social policy has established. Down with those evil institutions of cruelty and neglect. It's cheaper, too, to have even the most needy cared for at home by families whose own resources—both financial and emotional—are strained beyond imaginable limits. "You are not a bad mother if you place your special needs child," I would say. "Having a child living outside your home does not mean you are 'giving him up.'" In fact, we saw Zach frequently, brought him home in the years when he was still physically strong.

I spoke at conferences, at universities, at medical centers. The first time I spoke on television was in the spring of 1980. A producer had seen the story in Redbook, and she called me in Ames. They would fly me to Baltimore, Maryland where I would be a guest on a television show and talk about my family's decision.

I was watching television in the hotel room in Baltimore on the morning I was to be on and saw an advertisement for the show. There was our family picture from Redbook, splashed across screen. The deep voice-over said something about "one family's heartbreaking story..."

The program was called "People are Talking," WJZ-TV, a local talk-show, co-hosted by a middle-aged white man and a young, black woman. I had never been on television before and sharing this most intimate and sad story as a debut was daunting. "You don't have to be nervous," the male host assured me. "We'll ask all the questions and you just answer honestly."

I sat in a chair while someone from make-up applied blush. He told me that I had the same cheekbone structure as the actress Karen Black. I said "thank you," not knowing whether or not that was meant as a compliment. I had just turned thirty-four years old. My hair was recently permed and it was wildly untamed, perhaps unsuitable for my presentation as a bereaved mother. "What's your story, hon?" the make-up man asked. But before I could answer, I was hooked up with a microphone.

The two hosts of "People are Talking" were very nice and did a good job, especially the woman who, although single and childless, seemed to have such genuine empathy. She told me she cried reading the Redbook article and saw the picture of Zach. She took my hand and told me I was doing a good thing to go on television and share my story. She said how much my story could help other people, those women who also have a profoundly handicapped child. I don't remember the man's name from the show, but the woman's name was Oprah Winfrey. "You just tell your story as it is," she said, giving me confidence. That's what she seemed interested in: that sharing my story would help others.

It is difficult to explain to anyone who hasn't had a child like Zachariah the awful mixture of sorrow and relief that you feel when he dies. I had said that I did not want Zach to grow to be a man—a retarded man who would still be a baby in diapers, a man who needed to be shaved. But even though every normal milestone—a loose baby tooth, another birthday—was like a needle to the heart, I wasn't able to let him go. I always cheered for him when he pulled out of yet another high fever, survived another bout of pneumonia. Then I despaired, knowing that the event would soon repeat itself and devastate us all once again.

The last year of Zachariah's life he was so sick. The nurses at the children's home where he lived used to call me: "Come now. It's time." I would be on watch by his bedside, only to see his breathing stabilize, the color return to his face. Then I would kiss him and go back home, because it wasn't yet "time."

Zachariah was sixteen when he died. I had been with him the night before, but then I left to go home and sleep. I was not there with him early the next morning when he finally passed. It is one of the regrets of my life.

There's a wonderful short story by the writer Lorrie Moore called "Children Like That are the Only Children Here." The story is from the point of view of a young mother, a writer, whose baby is in the hospital, possibly with some form of cancer. The story, oddly self-conscious of the horrific nature of its subject matter, is at once dark and bitter, funny and searing. Moore describes another mother in the pediatric ward as talking of the "collateral beauty" one picks up along the way when going through the experience of caring for a damaged child. Although the story's narrator dismisses this notion, it is because she is too immersed in her own pain to see the truth in this observation.

I think this was so in my own life. Struck again and again, as I was, by the strength of ordinary people. I used to meet a group of women for morning coffee—we called ourselves "The Retarded Mothers' Coffee," and these women taught me lessons about endurance and humility and humor.

Because of Zachariah I have learned that children are from us, but they are separate from us. They are "loaners," here with us for a while before we give them up. Perfect or imperfect, we must let them go. Some we can send out into the world with all our hopes and dreams; proudly, we watch as they soar. Other children—the fragile, the damaged, the needy ones—we must make arrangements for; we hold our breath and pray that they can stay afloat. Sometimes these children leave us for good.

While having a child like Zachariah is not a blessing, I do believe that compassion, wisdom and strength can come from the experience. My senses are attuned always to the knowledge that healthy children, my grandchildren, are a miracle. It took a long time to recognize that. I was Zachariah's mother and eventually grateful for how my life changed, all that I learned and became because I had the chance to be Zachariah's mother. The collateral beauty, I suppose.

As I write this, I realize that Zachariah has been gone more years than he was alive. The milestones I used to record with some pain—he would be heading off to kindergarten, playing Little League in the spring, graduating from high school—don't stand out so vividly in my consciousness. It used to be hard to see my brother's son, Abram, who was born just two months after Zachariah, and envisioning what could have been. I don't feel this so strongly any more, and only a fleeting pang when I saw Abram, tall and handsome, walk down the aisle at his wedding last year. There are days that pass—perhaps weeks—when I do not think of Zach at all. There is nothing else, nothing new to say even if there remains always something of Zach with me, his essence, who he was.

The best is a really good dream, a dream that hangs sweetly about through the day, like the memory of a goodnight kiss. I had one such dream just the other night. I was in a bed and Zach—he was maybe five or six in the dream; he did not have the ravaged body of his sixteen-year-old self before he died. In the dream I am in the bedroom on Lynn Avenue, the house I shared with my first family. I am lying widthwise across the bed and holding Zach above me; his arms are resting on my chest; he's almost, not quite, supporting himself as he almost, not quite, could do when he was little. He's facing me—I can smell his baby breath—and he's laughing. Suddenly he says, "I'm here, Mama!" Just like that and proud as punch: "I'm here, Mama."

In the dream, I call to Zach's father who is in the bathroom down the hall. I hear someone peeing, hear the stream as it hits the bowl, so I call again over the sound: "Come in here, now!" Zach's dad—my first husband—comes in. He is wearing one of the outfits he used to wear around the house: sweat pants and a three-button, long sleeved, gray, cotton pullover. His hair is matted and he looks sleepy, as if, indeed, he just got up out of bed.

"Zachy just *said* something," I tell him, so excited that my heart is beating fast in my chest. I urge Zach: "Go ahead. Do it again." Zach is looking at me, still face to face, we are so close; there is a smear of drool along his cheek, but it is baby

Leaving Long Island...and other departures

drool, not the spittle of his older, handicapped self. "Come on, Zachy," I want him to speak. His father stands in the doorway, looking skeptical. Also, tired and annoyed, like he really doesn't believe me and just wants to get back in bed.

"I'm here, Mama," Zach says again, smiling so big. As if where else would he be?

In reality, it is Joe, my second husband, who has come back to bed from the bathroom. He climbs in beside me, gently nudging me over. "Are you awake, Sweetie?"

"Oh, I had the best dream," I tell him.

Joe pats my shoulder. Which means: *Save it for the morning.*

In a blink, he is sleeping, but I am still in a dreamy state, trying to get straight that I am not in the house on Lynn Avenue where I lived for almost twenty years with my first husband. Gabi, grown and gone, is not in the next bedroom with her stuffed animals and sleeping under a yellow checked comforter. For a moment, I am confused and think: Well, where *does* Zachariah sleep in *this* house? Which bedroom is he in? And then I remember where I am.

9

Once I was asked to write an article by a woman who was putting together an anthology about cross-cultural marriages. At first, I refused, saying I didn't believe that I was in a cross-cultural marriage. "Oh, aren't you a Jew, married to an Arab?" the woman asked.

Winter, 1990. Picture this: My second husband and I, married less than a year, are in Florida at a party for my parents' fiftieth wedding anniversary. In celebration of this achievement my parents are flying to Israel in a few days. Their lifelong friends are all at this party: Sylvia and Harold, Leona and Carl, Bernice and Harry. They are talking with great enthusiasm about Israel, about the trips they have all taken: one couple even attended a grandson's bar mitzvah in Israel, a family highlight.

My husband enters the conversation, an innocent. He says how he would *love* to go to Israel someday; he was so sorry not to have been able to visit when he was in the Middle East in the early Seventies. "In the Middle East without going to Israel?" someone clucks at the pity.

"I was in Egypt, in Syria, in Lebanon for a few weeks... before the civil war..." my husband goes on.

My parents' friends look puzzled: How could anyone go to the Middle East and not make Israel the prime destination? "So close and you didn't get to Israel?" someone else asks. "Why not?"

"Joe's not Jewish," I tell my parents' friends, gently letting them know that Israel doesn't have quite the same meaning. There is the assumption that because he is my husband, because he is short and dark and looks like a lot of the other men in the room—that, in fact, he looks like my father—that Joe is Jewish.

"Well, I wanted to go to Israel," my husband says. "I would love to have gone. But I couldn't."

The friends are immediately attentive. I hold my breath. "You *couldn't?*" someone finally responds. Now everyone looks totally confused. My husband goes on to explain that because he was *born* in Lebanon there was a problem. "You see, my passport was limited to..."

A hush falls over the room as I watch the looks on their faces. Confusing enough that my second husband had the same first name as my first, who many of my parents' friends had known since I was a teenager. Confusing enough that this was a man whom I said had sole custody of his young daughters (what could the mother have done?). Ok. So he wasn't Jewish. Their generation was just getting used to the mixed marriages, the divorces, a gay son or daughter. But this: Ruth and Milton's daughter had actually gone and married one of *them*. This short, swarthy man before them is—yes, he really is—an *Arab!*

But then what did a Jewish girl from Long Island know of Arabs? There were only images of them as enemies of Israel. No distinctions were made. Who knew from Syrians, Saudis, Lebanese; the Muslims, the Christians, the Melkites, the Shiites, the Copts, all seen together as a monolithic group. Arabs were *them*: an untrustworthy, rock-throwing people who wanted Israel destroyed. Arabs were who killed the Israeli athletes in Munich. Arabs were who threw grenades into busloads of school children. Even before 9/11, in those days before everyone knew and read a lot more about the Middle East, the word itself (ARAB!) seemed like a pejorative to many Jews.

My parents, Ruth and Milt, 1939

Joe Geha, Ruth, Fern, and Milt in Florida, 1990

The wedding invitations for my second marriage read: *Come join us as we exchange wedding vows and bravely blend our families.* We knew that courage would be a vital ingredient in this second family mix. Courage. And optimism. And commitment. A little family therapy wouldn't hurt either.

We had an outdoor wedding on the most beautiful day in June where everything was just bursting into bloom. Gabi was eighteen then; she walked me down the lawny aisle of a friend's backyard, both of us carrying backyard bouquets made by friends. I wore a white linen dress. Gabi said when I bought it: "White? You're not kidding anyone, Mom."

The groom, balding and middle-aged, was accompanied down the aisle by *his* two daughters. The Unitarian minister read a poem about marriage being a rose garden "where squash is fond to grow." We included the children in the ceremony. Joe and I made vows to each other and to our girls ("Because you are the daughter of the one I love. . ."); we exchanged rings.

I was nervous, of course. The Valium I had taken, along with a few sips of champagne before the ceremony, made me appear a little cock-eyed in the wedding video. I loved Joe for his gentleness, his loyalty, his humor. But I also had *qualms*. The notion of living with someone else's preadolescent children is enough to give anyone qualms. *Especially* if you've had a child yourself and know the commitment needed to turn out a reasonably successful human being. To say nothing of the hours of car-pooling.

We were both over forty. Both of us, too, had lived through some hard times. To say that in middle age we came into this new relationship with old baggage is an understatement. We came packed with steamer trunks—which is just the way Joe came to this country in the first place.

Joseph Albert (Yousef Abdullah) Geha was born in 1944 in Zahle, Lebanon, a mountain town high above the Bekaa valley, halfway between Damascus and Beirut. After World War II, his father packed up a young wife and three children and came to America, where they lived above the grocery store that he opened in Toledo, Ohio, with money saved from years of peddling dry goods.

Joe didn't speak English until the first grade when his father dropped him off at a Catholic school and left, never telling Joe that he'd be back. One of the first complete English sentences that Joe remembers was hissed into his ear by an Ursuline nun: "Stop crying or I'll give you something to cry about!"

In elementary school, he was teased for his accent, called "dirty A-rab," and embarrassed by the strange foods his mother put in his lunch box—the leftover ground lamb with cinnamon, the sweet greens cooked down in olive oil and rolled into paper-thin *lawash* bread. He insisted that he no longer be called "Zuzu"—the Arabic diminutive for Yousef—but "Joe," a solidly American name. He longed to be a real American. To eat peanut butter and jelly sandwiches on Wonder Bread. To have parents who understood things like Cub Scouts and baseball and the PTA.

Keenly, all through his childhood and adolescence, he felt the difference. And even though he was the first in his family to graduate from college—and went on to become a writer and a college professor himself—the difference, the sense of himself as an outsider, I think, remained. Though he *has* come to appreciate his roots now—certainly the culinary ones. I eat with enthusiasm the foods of his childhood, the food he makes with the recipes handed down from all the women in the family. Once we got a package in the mail, the brown wrapper dripping with honey: Baklava from Aunt Sophie in Detroit. There was no accompanying note. Aunt Sophie can cook but she cannot write English. In our spice cabinet there is a homemade mix: Aunt Maheeba's special blend of cumin and cinnamon and coriander. Years ago, Joe visited his mother in the hospital after her heart attack. He had brought her some *sfeehas,* Lebanese spinach pies, which he had made from her recipe. Among her last words to him before her death were: "Next time, more lemon."

Comedian Lenny Bruce used to have a routine in which he made the distinction between *goyish* and Jewish: trailer parks and lime Jell-O and the Marine Corps are *goyish*; condos and rye bread and accounting are Jewish; everyone in the Midwest is gentile, even if they're not; everyone in New York is Jewish, even if they're not. Especially Italians. Italians are very Jewish, Bruce said. And so, might I add, are Arabs. Which is why Joe and I seem so at home in each other's skin. As if we come from the same place.

To illustrate, here's another story with my parents living in Florida when Joe and I were visiting one time, early in our new marriage: Joe is in the bathroom, but the door is open, and he is rummaging through the medicine chest looking for the sinus medication I put away. From the hall, I hear him and ask if he is looking for aspirin. "No," he calls back. "I'm just taking one of these." In the doorway, he shakes the prescription bottle.

"What's he taking?" calls my mother from the kitchen.

"He's taking a pill?"

Then my father yells in from the bedroom: "Is he sick? What's the matter with him? What's he taking?" If my grandparents were still alive, they too would be calling, from their respective places in the house.

Joe looks at me and smiles. "I feel as if I'm back on Monroe Street," he says. Monroe Street is where he lived with his family above the store.

It's the intrusiveness, I think. A kind of well-meaning busybodiness that characterized both our homes and separated Joe and me from the more emotionally remote families—the ones my family called *goyisha*, what Joe's referred to as *Amerkani*.

I had known Joe Geha for years as a friend. He was in the English department where I had done graduate work and occasionally taught part-time. Often we were at the same parties and always gravitated together to talk. For a few years he was in a writers' group I belonged to that met once a month. I was married then to my first husband. I thought happily but what did I know? Later Joe told me that when the writers' group met at his house, he had cleaned all day just to impress me—though I don't recall being impressed by his housekeeping.

Single for too long after his divorce, taking care of daughters on his own, a nice guy like that should be married, my friends and I agreed. Once I introduced Joe to a single friend at a party. Later that week I called him and asked whether or not he had asked her out. He was reluctant. "She looks like the women in my family," he said, although I found her beauty dark and exotic. "He's too short," my friend said, when I told her that I had given Joe her phone number.

For a couple of years, one of my best friends was his officemate. Nancy and I had many conversations, putting our heads together about who to fix Joe Geha up with. It was Nancy who saved him from almost marrying the wrong woman. Joe had an older student, a divorced woman with three children in one of his classes. When the semester ended, she called him, inviting him for a Christmas dinner. She made homemade fried chicken, she read Kafka, she had long, blonde hair. Bamboozled is the word that comes to mind, for within six weeks, she had set a marriage date. Perhaps she did love him. Those who knew her thought she wanted a way out of a struggling single-parent existence.

One day, Nancy—a brave woman who speaks her mind—was getting ready to go home for the day. Joe had just come in from a class, and as Nancy got on her coat, she backed him up against the bookshelf. "I'm going to say this once and then I'll never say anything else to you about it again," she said, pointing a finger at his chest. "If you marry this woman, you'll be making the mistake of your life!"

Well, there's nothing you do after saying something like that except make a dramatic and speedy exit. Nancy turned on her heel and Joe was left, his mouth agape. Nancy had planted a seed of doubt. The faster the relationship headed toward union—with talk of houses and down payments and reserving the hall—the colder his feet got. At night he had dreams that he couldn't swallow and had to pull out the long, blonde hair that was stuck down his throat. When he told his fiancée that "this was moving a little too quickly," she became angry, gave him an ultimatum. Marriage this summer or nothing at all, she said. And so it was—nothing at all.

Joe is forever indebted to Nancy for letting him know what she thought of his impending marriage. Just as grateful as I am. Two years later, when my marriage blew apart, Joe Geha was a friend and a source of comfort. Once I called him up to set up a writers' meeting. "How *are* you?" he asked, concern registering in his voice. We talked for hours. I told him I had just begun to see a therapist. He offered to tell me everything *he* had learned in therapy, "so I could save you the money," he said jokingly. I knew he had just ended a relationship with a woman. "Do you want to go out for dinner sometime" I asked just before we hung up. "How about tonight?" he said.

•

"Is this a *date?*" Gabi asked when I told her I was going out. A date! The word sent shivers through me. After years of couple's bridge and wearing socks to bed, how was I ever going to start *dating* again? I was forty-two years old. I had cesarean scars and fresh incisions along my left breast where I had just had two lumps removed. Watching me undress one night, my daughter remarked kindly: "Mom, you have a very nice body, and the scars make you look *experienced*."

"A date?" I repeated dumbly. "No, we're just friends. "

But I came home from dinner that night and thought, "OK, I'll marry him." I told this to no one. Of course, Joe hadn't asked. He kept thinking that he was giving comfort and advice to a friend. In fact, months later, when I told Gabi that I was planning to get married, she asked: "Does Joe know yet?"

I just *knew*. That's all there was to it. We went out as friends and we were immediately as comfortable and kind together as lifetime companions. Perhaps it is a spin on love at first sight. Seeing someone who is a friend in a whole new light. For years I had plotted with Nancy to fix up this man with a suitable woman. And then there I was. We read the same books. We made each other laugh. We started so slowly, going out for a couple of months before we slept together. And then it was my idea—I'm not sure how long it would have taken him to ask. I was assured by the ease and pleasure of it—how well we seemed to fit, how completely I trusted myself to him. Although I admit I was shocked to see he was uncircumcised, so that the first thought I had was of my grandfather rolling over in his grave. Papa would shake his head: "Fernie, *Trafe!*"

Sometime soon after Joe and I were more than "just friends," I was helping him clean up the dinner dishes at his house, and I noticed something on the wall, a strange plastic utensil with backward cut-out letters, "What's this?" I asked, holding it up.

"It's a toast press," he told me. "When I make cinnamon toast in the morning for the girls...." Then he demonstrated by putting some bread in the toaster and holding the press against the warmed slice. Imprinted in the toast were the words: I LOVE YOU.

"And I do, you know," he said, smearing the toast with sugar and cinnamon and cutting off a buttery piece for me.

"What?"

"I do love you." He added seriously: "I would never cheat or lie to someone I made a promise to. I would be faithful to you always."

Megan and Katie were with their mother for the weekend, so we rented movies, brought in wood for the fireplace and drank wine. We stayed up half the night and talked and talked. He mused about what would have happened to us if we had met when we were young. "I've always had close women friends, but often when there was a woman I was attracted to, I was too shy to ask her out," he confessed.

Joe Geha and I had been in college at the same time during the Sixties: he, attending a city university in Ohio; I, a state school in New York. His family—a mother and father both of whom could barely read English and who had not more than three years of formal education between them—expected that their child would go to college, make something of himself. Why else all those years of standing behind a cash register fourteen hours a day in a grocery store? When, as a university professor, Joe had a book of short stories published, he sent a copy to his mother. Although she was unable to read it, she was proud to see her son's picture on the back.

In college both of us had been English majors. This meant that we both read what had been the canon at the time: Hemingway, Fitzgerald, T.S. Eliot, Faulkner. We both wrote term papers on *Death of a Salesman*. He wrote a short story about his passage from Lebanon, about how his older sister had typhoid fever, and how his father had to pinch her cheeks to give them color so no one would know the family had a sick child before he boarded the ship for America. I told him about my short story about Papa leaving Russia.

Joe and I followed that writer's adage: write what you know. And we followed the prescribed English major curriculum and read what they told us to. And all of those years that we were reading and writing the same kinds of things helped to create a shared backdrop of aesthetic experience and historical reference.

Suddenly, I could picture us together in college, having a soda together in the student union, cutting classes because we were having so much fun in each other's company, going to foreign films and then talking about how pretentious they were. And he would have been a good friend, there for me always, a comfortable shoulder to cry on when the boy I was in love with—a boy like my ex-husband—behaved badly.

I think sometimes how mothers can warn their daughters about certain kinds of men. What do we tell them? That there are the stars, the football heroes, the brooding boys whom you will try, without success, to make happy. These are the boys who have too much anger at the world, and some of it will be taken out on you. These are the boys whose sense of entitlement encourages unfaithfulness. And these are not the boys you should marry.

There are other gentler boys who don't win at every game or shine from across a crowded room. They are not macho or rock star gorgeous. These are the boys who notice you before you notice them; the boys who are sometimes a little silly but who always make you laugh; the boys who drive sensibly and are kind to their little brothers and sisters. These are the boys you should marry.

"When I was young, I wasn't ready for the kind of man you are," I told him.

Fern Kupfer and Joe Geha, 2007

10

"I have some reading I'd like you to do," I told Dr. Tim Leeds. I brought him my file. It was growing bigger every day. There was all the information the genetics department had given me. And the articles I found on the Internet about the BRCA gene and hereditary cancers. If I were a doctor, I would appreciate a patient like me: someone who reads the medical literature and asks a lot of questions. I suppose there are doctors who think patients like me are a pain in the ass.

Joe plays poker with doctors. The game started in the early 90s when a friend of ours asked Tim (an ob-gyn) who lived down the street, who asked Jay (an allergist) who asked John (a pediatrician) who asked Ken (an ophthalmologist) if they wanted to start a regular poker game. Mark (a surgeon) comes on occasion, as does Selden (a neurologist). Word got around the doctor's lounge, and this became a very popular Friday night poker game. At this point in his life, Joe says he wouldn't mind if the regulars were joined by a urologist and a cardiologist.

The poker game is good-humored, and the stakes are low. These doctors are pretty much guys who share each other's political and social sensibilities. Jay had started the free clinic in town. A number of the docs do volunteer work in other countries. For a number of years Joe went to the Dominican Republic to help with a "tubal team," a dozen or so volunteers from the States—nurses, obstetrician-gynecologists, pharmacologists, anesthesiologists. And my husband, a retired English professor.

This began after one game several years ago when Joe casually mentioned that he'd like to do a "little volunteer work" when he retired. Tim Leeds immediately spoke up: the surgical team he volunteered for would soon be making its annual trip to the Dominican Republic. They really could use an extra hand. Joe would have to pay his own way. My husband was skeptical. He didn't know if his many years of hypochondria would count as medical training.

Tim explained that the mission hospital down there didn't have an autoclave; all surgical instruments had to be cleaned and sterilized manually. By signing on, Joe would free a medically trained team member to do more specialized work. In other words, they could use a dishwasher. Joe thought, after a long career of reading student papers, scrubbing bloody surgical instruments might be a welcome change.

The women were Haitians, most of them, and the poorest of the Dominican Republic's poor; many had been sneaked in illegally across the border, lured by *buscones* or recruiters promising work in the sugar cane fields. It's a kind of serfdom: back-breaking work, dirt floor shacks without running water, communities, called *bateys*, remotely located in the midst of the cane fields.

The women of the *bateys* often started getting pregnant as teenagers. By the time the medical team saw them they were in their twenties and thirties, and they come after seven, eight, ten, *fourteen* pregnancies. Not all the children survive. Nor do all the mothers.

One year the nurses were talking about how they tried to do the math, figuring how many unwanted pregnancies had been prevented, and by extension how many down the line. It was daunting, and they soon gave up counting. Doing such math is baffling, exhausting in the face of how much more needed to be done. The motto of the tubal team: change the world one woman at a time.

But it's not like the tubal team doesn't have a good time. After a hard day in the operating rooms, there's drinking the local cold brew: Presidente beer. One time Joe drank too much, fell asleep in his clothes, and woke to find his toenails painted bright red. "The nurses," he explained to me when he went into town to call home. "But Tim took care of me; gave me crackers and aspirin before I fell asleep."

Dr. Timothy Leeds is not only Joe's poker buddy, but also our good friend. He likes to take care. An extroverted Irish storyteller, a practicing Catholic, a lover of good food and drink, Tim is an energetic, can-do kind of guy. Much of this he attributes to his recently self-diagnosed ADHD. When his very bright—but not studiously focused—sons were found to have attention deficit, Tim decided he did, too. Now he's on a mission: he diagnoses women in labor, friends with marital problems, our daughter, Megan: Attention Deficit Disorder.

Tim loves both women and babies and lots of movement, so being an ob-gyn with hyperactivity is a good fit. He is always picking up someone's baby and willing to talk shop with anyone about hormone replacement or fertility treatments. When, because of early contractions, Gabi was on bed-rest during the last months of her second pregnancy, she called every time the poker game was at our house to talk with Tim. So when I was talking about all the decisions I had to make because of the BRCA gene, he said: "Let's do it!" Meaning, he wanted to take out my ovaries.

"Right now? Before dessert?" I asked.

He and his wife, Barb, were over for dinner that night. Barb is a fabulous cook—as is my husband—and we have shared some terrific meals over the years. That night, Joe had grilled shish-kabob with marinated lamb. Barb had brought over homemade ginger ice cream.

Tim is not my regular doctor, but some years ago, when Dr. Amin found a growth on my cervix, I asked Tim if he would be comfortable seeing me as a patient. The question was not so much if *he* would be comfortable, but if I would. Tim scheduled me in the next day. He enjoys that privilege: getting his friends in. It's like giving us a VIP pass to get into the executive lounge. I was surprised that I felt comfortable having a pelvic exam by someone I saw socially. "I'll just clip this little sucker off," Tim said confidently, before I could even ask if anesthesia would be involved. His nurse rolled her eyes, as if: *see what I have to put up with from this guy.*

Tim always wears red Converse sneakers to work, his lucky footwear. On the wall of his examination room there is a framed photograph of a tiny newborn wrapped in a blanket inside a big, red sneaker.

The article that I'd like Tim to read is from the FORCE website: *Ovarian Cancer Risk Reduction. One study showed a 96% risk reduction for ovarian cancer after prophylactic oophorectomy. A recent study of 122 BRCA positive women undergoing prophylactic oophorectomy found that about 6% of these women had cancer at the time of the prophylactic surgery.*

This panics me. The idea that I would be perfectly healthy going in to an operation that might not be necessary and ovarian cancer would be discovered. "That seems high," I say to Tim. "Six percent already have ovarian cancer?"

It was a lovely Sunday afternoon in May before the bugs were out in full force. Nothing is nicer than a beautiful spring day in Iowa—except maybe most of the year in San Diego. Because there are not too many flawless, warm, blue-skied mosquito-less days, Iowans appreciate them all the more. I had set out hanging baskets of petunias and geraniums, filled pots with marigolds and rock roses. We were sitting on the back deck having white wine and stuffed mushroom caps.

"You don't have ovarian cancer, Fern," Tim assured me. He said that he has never, ever, performed a prophylactic surgery and discovered cancer. I don't know if he is telling the truth. Yes, you want your surgeon to be confident. But how many BRCA positive women were here in central Iowa? Also how many prophylactic surgeries has he done? Barbara on Long Island would want to know. "Always ask how many operations of this kind the doctor does," she reminds me.

"There are certain protocols for BRCA positive women," I said. I started talking about peritoneal wash and read aloud from the article: *It is important to be certain that the surgeon performing the prophylactic oophorectomy is familiar with the associated fallopian tube risk in BRCA carriers and that the pathology department that reviews the ovaries performs what is known as a 'serial sectioning' where they look at many cross sections of the fallopian tubes to be certain that a cancer is not present.*

Tim nodded, ok, ok, as if this was all not news to him. He drew me pictures of fallopian tubes and ovaries on a napkin.

I asked: "Do you think I should go to Mayo? Should I have a gynecological oncologist do this surgery?"

Tim told me that he would not be the least insulted if I didn't choose him to do this surgery.

"Would you feel relieved *not* to do the surgery on a friend?"

No, he would like to do the procedure. "But you have to do what you feel comfortable with, Fern."

Dinner was ready, but we continued to talk about laparoscopy vs. laparotomy. Hysterectomy and removal of the uterus. Barb was quiet and patient. Being the wife of an ob-gyn, I imagine, had interrupted their social lives on more than this cocktail conversation.

Tim said, "You want me to take your uterus out, I will. But it's not necessary. He went on to assure me that the risk of uterine cancer among BRCA positive women is the same as the general population. There are risks with this additional surgery. And there are obvious signs to signal uterine cancer.

Taking out tubes and ovaries would not be difficult, Tim assured me. I was past menopause. Not exactly as if I still needed these parts. I shouldn't have any hormonal reactions. "You had an easy menopause, right?" Tim asked. (There had been many a poker night when I had taken Tim from the card table to talk about hot flashes and hormone replacement.)

The average age for women to go through menopause was fifty-two. I was fifty-two when my mother died in the spare bedroom in our home in Iowa. She had come back from Florida to live with us once again. I remember one night, when she turned to Joe after dinner: "You know, the food's so good here. I don't think I'm going to die so fast." Strange, that after my mom died a month later, I never had another period. Just like that, it ended, once and for all.

"What about doing both procedures—the oophorectomy and the mastectomies at the same time?" I asked. I still could not say the words "double mastectomy" without my knees going weak. That was the part I just couldn't easily face. I poured myself another glass of wine. Tim finished his Scotch.

The week before I had spoken with a woman I met on the FORCE website. She was just a few years younger than I and was having both procedures done at once. In part because she said she was a "chicken" and wanted everything over with at once. Also because she could only take six weeks sick leave and keep her job.

No, Tim wouldn't recommend doing both operations at once. Neither would Mark Taylor, another poker player. And, in everyone's opinion, one of the best surgeons around. Not just in Iowa. The gynecological part is a 'dirtier' operation. More chance for infection if the breasts are done at the same time. The patient would also be under anesthesia much longer. That's riskier, too. But then again, so is going under two separate times.

Uterus in. Breasts off. Maybe next summer, not this. Here in Ames or at the Mayo clinic? Go and stay with Barbara in New York? I could do this. I could do that. Is there a pressing rush to make these decisions besides the fact that sleep eludes me, and I can hardly think of anything else?

Tim wanted me to meet a BRCA-positive woman who has been a patient of his for some years. He had delivered her children. Recently he performed a hysterectomy on her. She was going to have her breasts removed next month, after she was completely recovered from the hysterectomy. Tim said he would call and ask if she would speak with me. "I'm sure she will."

"What procedures has she done? Why a hysterectomy and not an oophorectomy..." My questions were endless.

Joe was already passing a basket of warm bread; Barb had tossed the salad.

Tim stopped, just looked at me, indicating that, because of confidentiality, he would say no more. "Talk to her. Diana will tell you everything," he said.

"Diana? That's her name? Diana?"

His wife flashed him a warning look. Tim shouldn't have said her name without permission. Tim has given my name to women who have had handicapped children. I have always given him permission, always grateful to share. Tim respects the way women talk to each other. He has said that although he loves babies, he would never go into this specialty if he were going to medical school all over again. Women want to go see a woman. "You're really going to like Diana," he told me. "She's a lot like you: smart, assertive." He added: "I'm a little afraid of her, actually."

I asked the "what would you do if I were your wife" question. Should I go to Mayo Clinic? Should I go to New York as Barbara wants me to do. Tim, whose flesh-and-blood wife was sitting across from me at the table, revealed that he would have her stay in Ames, do a prophylactic oophorectomy—which could be done laproscopically. "And you know how much I love my wife," he said with a mischievous grin, topping off his drink.

A few days before, Gabi had gone to the clinic at Northwestern and had herself tested for the BRCA gene. She doesn't procrastinate, gets things done. But now there was another immediate thing to worry about. She would find out the results the week I was in Long Island for the high school reunion. I was so distracted I could not think clearly myself.

"Let's look at this positively," Tim said. "You don't have cancer. You're lucky."

Yes, I am going to look at this positively. Talk myself up before the big game. I am lucky, lucky, lucky. I don't have cancer (Tim says). Knowledge is power. Or maybe ignorance is bliss. Pick the cliché that works for you.

Leaving Long Island...and other departures

11

From: Diana
To: Fern
Subject: BRCA 1

Dear Fern,
I am sorry for your BRCA 1 news, but it helps to know that there are others out there going through the same process.

I can tell from our phone conversation that you love life, and I do too! We will take this journey together.

OK then, see you Thurs. at 10am at The Café. I am a fairly small, blond (or at least like to pretend that I'm still blond!). I've seen your picture on a book cover, so I think I'll find you. Diana

It's as if I've signed onto a very unusual dating service: coffee with Mary Anne, emails with Lucy; phone calls with Sally in Wisconsin. I reach out, even though we might have nothing in common besides a cancer mutation or mastectomy. It is the same thing I used to do when I was defined as Zachariah's mother. Make that cold call. "You don't know me but…" How do you get through this? We are in an exclusive sorority that no woman would want to join.

    I had decided to have the oophorectomy first, when I returned from the high school reunion. Making the decisions about the prophylactic mastectomies was scarier, and I wanted to talk with more people. Last week I had a date with Carol, set up by a woman in my bridge group.

    I was already in Stomping Grounds, a local coffee shop near campus, when Carol arrived. Carol does not have the BRCA gene, but last year had a double mastectomy following chemotherapy for a particularly invasive cancer. Carol is a scientist at the university; even in middle age she has the alert look of the smartest girl in class. "Fern?" She put her hand on my shoulder and then sat across from me. We started talking about breasts before the waitress even poured the water into our glasses.

Carol's reconstructive surgery followed almost a year after the conclusion of her chemotherapy treatments, "I didn't think I was going to do it. I had gone through so much, I didn't want to go back and do any more medical procedures. But it turns out, I'm very glad I did." Carol was encouraging. She had the Deep Inferior Epigastric Perforator surgery, the most state-of-the-art breast reconstruction surgery available. The DIEP is a fairly new procedure, an intensive microsurgery which uses your own belly fat to create new breasts. The good thing is that there is not a foreign substance (like saline or silicone) inside you. The downside is that this is a complicated surgery with a longer recovery time.

Carol was very pleased with the result. "My pants actually fit better," she said. "My waist is smaller and my stomach is flatter than it's been in years." She pulled the band across the top of her pants to show the fit.

The idea seemed appealing. Belly is one of the few places I have excess. Too skinny when I was a kid, my mom made me drink "guggle-muggles," malteds with cream and raw eggs. As a teenager, I would sit by the side of the swimming pool in Plainview, flattening my thighs against the concrete to make the top of my legs appear fleshier. One summer—I was about fourteen then— and wearing the shortest, tightest jean shorts, I wiggled my little behind in front of a bunch of teenage boys leaning against a car: "Hey, toothpick legs," one of them called out as I walked by.

But for most of my adult life clothes fit easily, shopping was fun. I liked my body. Not completely—no woman ever does. But mini-skirts were fun to wear (I have a photo of me student teaching, standing at the blackboard in front of a junior high English class. I couldn't lift my arms above shoulder height, that's how short the skirt was). Junior size five—except for later during the pregnancies. And then I felt powerful, taking up more space.

For years, you see your physical self in an unchanging way, but in my late forties I had an epiphany about how my body had aged. Walking downtown on a summer day, I saw a reflection in the vestibule of a store window. The image was coming right towards me. The woman's walk was purposeful, arms swinging. She was thin but there was certainly the beginning of a potbelly. I had a flashing thought: "What is my mother doing here?" But the woman was me.

Belly fat to breasts. What a neat idea. I could garner a good size "B" cup from my mid-section. Maybe more. "Would you like to see me?" Carol asked, after we had finished our half sandwich and soup. We paid the check and walked to the women's bathroom in the back hallway. There was a college girl at the sink washing her hands as Carol and I approached the handicapped stall and went in together.

Carol unbuttoned her shirt. "These scars will fade more, but I think it looks pretty good now," she said. Her new breasts, created from her old belly were small and natural looking. Unremarkable, except for the fact that there were no nipples. Creating nipples was an additional surgery and Carol said in her no-nonsense way that she didn't particularly care about having nipples. It looked a little strange. As if her breasts were blind.

"I was in intensive care for a few days," Carol admitted. Then she told me about how long the operation was, the complications. Apparently, her plastic surgeon was wonderful and actually ended up staying with her through the night in the hospital.

"Intensive care?" I repeated.

"It was difficult, but now I think it was worth it," she said. "I'm definitely glad I did it."

The next day I meet Diana, the woman Tim Leeds connected me to. Diana is a history teacher at a junior high in a small town a few miles out of Ames. Diana emailed and suggested that we meet at 10:00 between breakfast and lunch, thinking that the Café, one of the most popular restaurants in Ames, wouldn't be so crowded at that time, and we could sit for a while. The Café is in a section of town that developers designed with a kind of new urbanism in mind: a planned mixture of row houses, private homes, apartments and commercial development. This seemed like a good idea, but it hasn't quite taken off, so the streets have the feel of a stage set, still with empty storefronts and vacant lots.

The woman I think must be Diana is already there in the front wearing a pink and black "Girl Power" tee shirt and carrying a large loose-leaf notebook; she looks both official and adorable. "You're Fern?" she asks and opens her arms. We hug, old friends who have never met. "Diana?" Tears come to my eyes. *I know you...*

And this I already know from our phone calls. When Diana was eight years old, she lost her mother to breast cancer. There was a family history of cancers. But it was the image of her own daughter without a mother—without her, Diana—that made Diana get genetic testing. She was positive for the BRCA 1 gene, although a different mutation from my own. Diana is not Jewish. In fact, she is the proverbial *shiksa* of any guy's dreams: long, straight blond hair, big blue eyes, a small, nearly perfect nose. She looks as if she just finished cheerleading practice.

I can't remember what we ate. Or even everything we talked about. The trajectory of our conversation went the way that the intimate talk of women often does. We meandered through our lives; revealed our secrets, our fears; we made jokes about sex; bragged about our children, we cried talking about our mothers. Tim Leeds had already completed her hysterectomy but it was not the easy-breezy recovery I was anticipating for myself. Not outpatient. And because Diana was young and pre-menopausal, she was going through a difficult emotional time following the operation. She thought of herself as a strong woman, a person whom others went to for help. She didn't like being seen as the needy one. Me, too, I said. Humility was never my strong suit. I told Diana how I didn't like it when I'd take Zach in his wheelchair through the mall, how I'd see the sorrowful looks in people's eyes. Don't feel sorry for me; I'm feeling sorry enough for myself, I wanted to say.

Diana shows me photographs of her most beautiful family. Her husband Jim is strong-jawed, muscled, summer-tanned. Her kids, blond and athletic, could pose for a Norman Rockwell calendar. "That's my Jade," Diana says. Pre-teen princess and soccer queen. "Jade knows everything that goes on. She's a worrier. But she's amazing. My best friend. I know I'm doing the right thing. I look at my daughter and I'm sure. I'm going to be here for her. Her high school graduation. Her wedding." Diana set her chin stubbornly. "I am not going to miss those things."

Next month, Diana is having her mastectomies and immediately beginning breast reconstruction, using silicone.

She doesn't have enough fat to create new breasts from her own body. Mark Taylor is doing the mastectomy here in Ames; she has interviewed plastic surgeons and the one she has chosen will come up to Ames from Des Moines and be in the operating room here during the surgery to put in the expanders. "I'm definitely going bigger." Diana is tiny. Her own breasts—the still healthy breasts she is removing—are barely an 'A' cup. "Jim says he doesn't care, but I think—might as well get something out of this." She tells me that when they made love the other night, her husband did not go near her breasts. "I said, 'go ahead, you can still touch them.'" She understands that his reluctance was out of sensitivity to her. They have a strong marriage; one in which she clearly calls the shots. She knows how much he loves her. She sighs: "Poor guy, he doesn't know what to do."

I don't think of my own breasts as a particular sexual part of me, nor is my female identity connected to them—maybe because I developed late. And my BRCA diagnosis came when I was already over sixty years old. But how would I feel without breasts? With reconstruction, I wouldn't go any larger than my normal breasts. But I wouldn't mind ones that did not give way to gravitational fall. Having the DIEP procedure would mean that new breasts would be created from my own body—so natural sagging would develop with time. And ending up in intensive care just to have sixty-year old saggy boobs? Although silicone is a foreign substance, the aesthetic appeal is stronger. Also an implant is not such a serious operation. "It *would* be nice never to wear a bra again. To just have some perky, high breasts, throw on a t-shirt and go," I muse.

Diana shows me a picture of some of the silicone breasts she has in her folder. "I wonder how they're going to be when

I run," she says. "People say that they just stay in place, they don't move. "

"Well, I don't think they're going to hit you in the chin."

"I can't believe that I'm really going to do this," she says.

That night I talk to a woman from Ohio whom I met in a chat room on the FORCE web site. She is going in for her mastectomy the next week, but has decided not to have any reconstruction at all. The simpler, the better, she says. She is older, like me, past menopause, married to the same man for almost forty years. "I'm not sure at this point, he would even know the difference." She wants to get back to work and to her gardening. "Who cares?" she says with a healthy irreverence. "My breasts were useful, I nursed my babies with them. But that time is over. I didn't keep the crib, did I?"

12

At the Plainview High School reunion, people were curious how I ended up living in Iowa. "Really, Iowa?" people asked in both good humor and amazement. "How far are you from Chicago? Iowa—you mean where the potatoes grow?"

Somehow the fortieth slipped by, so this high school reunion would be our forty-fifth. Barbara emailed me the news of divorces, marriages, deaths. Louis Brodsky is compiling surveys to be filled out. Recent pictures of us appear next to our yearbook photos. There we were. Our lives. Here we are. There are Plainview High School alums who became bikers or raised horses or who work in homeland security. We are entrepreneurs. Computer techs. We are teachers—many of us female because that's what the guidance counselors said smart girls could be in 1964. We are single, divorced, remarried, widowed. Some reconnected with old sweethearts. Some served in Vietnam. A few died there.

There are doctors and lawyers and, if not Indian chiefs, then certainly CEOs. Some of Plainview High School's best and brightest have made discoveries of things that I couldn't begin to explain. There are PHS alumni who own car washes and translation services and summer camps. We live on the land in the Northwest and in co-ops on the West Side. We made our homes on Long Island and California and Washington; Maui and London and Israel and Iowa.

I have brought some capris, which used to be called pedal-pushers in 1964. And some sweaters, something warm, because Barbara has warned me that there won't be heaters at the camp where the reunion will be held, and remember that May on Long Island can be quite cold.

"What are you wearing?" Barbara often asks when I come to New York. It is one of the things that I do not have to think about too much in Iowa. In winter we put on lots and lots of layers: Cuddle-duds and turtle-necks and cardigans and scarves. In summer, we take them off. When I pack to go to New York, I never have anything to wear. The suggested dress for the reunion held at The Driftwood Day Camp is casual. The camp in Melville, Long Island, is owned by our high school friend, Ronnie, who is generously hosting the event.

Barbara meets me at La Guardia. She is always the first person I see upon entering the terminal. In the old days, before security considerations made this impossible, Barbara would be working her way into the jetway tunnel as soon as it attached to the plane. Now she is safely behind the *ticketed passengers only* sign.

"Sweetie, you look good," she says, before hugging and hugging me. Assuring me that despite what I've told her, the worry and tension don't show as much as she might have thought. Approving of my outfit, a black and white shirt dress with a loose belt, black sandals with little heels, she gives a little nod. "Nice." She adds: "Oh, I love you, I love you, love you," Barbara often repeats things three times for emphasis. We are both crying. "It's going to be ok," she says. Then: "Shit! Shit! Shit!"

Barbara has just had her hair done, her usual mane now blown and straightened, the color lighter than the very dark brunette that was the original hue. Her manicure is perfect. I had my very first manicure when I was over forty, and Barbara took me to a Great Neck salon. None of the women there could believe that I had never had a professional manicure. "Well, she lives in Iowa," Barbara told everyone in the salon. As if I just drove in on the combine.

Barbara was a cheerleader who cried when Plainview High School lost a basketball game. Now she is a golfer who talks about her score. I never did get sports. She once took me to a Knicks game when I was in New York. "These tickets are wasted on you," she said as I looked more at the crowd than the court.

How have we managed all these years to be so absolutely committed to one another? We are life-long friends in good times and in bad, in sickness and in health. This is what a friend should be, I have always told my daughters when they were having difficulties with the cruelty of girls. There were times, many, when Barbara and I fought, but we have never been jealous or resentful of the good in each other's lives; never, ever not been joyous for the other's happiness.

"I'm not in such good shape," I tell her. The BRCA news weighs so heavily on me, the feeling of dread rises ominously when my mind wanders—about what I will do, about what will happen to Gabi. To Ruthie.

Gabi has just been tested. We are waiting for the news. If Gabi is positive for the BRCA gene, Ruthie will not be tested. Not yet. She is only six. There is nothing to be gained from dwelling on this now and it is emotionally destructive to go there. I have willed myself to stop thinking about it. Not always successfully. Gabi will know soon enough. Then I want to be strong to help with the decisions she would have to make.

My mother has been gone for ten years. I think of how terrible she would feel to think that she had passed us this genetic inheritance. Yet, Gabi, Ruthie and I also inherited her confidence, her outgoing personality, the sense of fun she brought coming into the room. My mom was ever optimistic, even at the end of her life when we looked for nursing homes near me in Iowa. I told her that there was a Jewish home in Des Moines, but in the newer ones, closer by, there were no Jews. Living always in Jewish communities, from the Bronx to Long Island to Florida, would she find that odd? No, she assured me. She found "gentiles very interesting." Besides: *You know, Fernie, where ever I go, people seem to like me.*

Barbara's car still smells new. She drives (always too fast for me) on the Long Island Expressway and merges with the assumption that others will make room for her. "What's going on here?" she says. There is heavy traffic. Barbara always appears both surprised and aggravated by traffic. "How are you doing?"

"I actually feel a little sick," I tell Barbara. "Like I'm coming down with something."

"You don't have to do anything. We'll go home, get into pajamas. You can read and relax in my bed," Barbara says. "The reunion is going to be amazing."

I know that the reunion will be a distraction. But what to say to those whom I have not seen since the last reunion in 1984? Plainview High School, class of 1964. The Gulls, our mascot. We are all in our sixties. *How are you? How are you? How are you?* I could say: *I moved to Iowa. I had two children. One of them had a deteriorating brain disease. I became a writer. I divorced. I remarried. I got tenure. I raised two stepdaughters. My son died. Here's a picture of my two grandchildren. I was just diagnosed with the BRCA gene. Next week I will take out my insides. Then I will take off my breasts.* Everyone has something.

We drive down Northern Boulevard, turning left onto a tree-lined street. It is a familiar route to me even though I never drive on Long Island. I didn't get my license until after I had graduated from college and lived in upstate New York. In this neighborhood of older, wealthy homes, stop sign after stop sign on each block makes the street safe enough to wheel a baby carriage down it. There are some young families again in this long established neighborhood. Great Neck is changing. What used to be an enclave for the descendants of Eastern European Jewry, are now Persians and Asians. Some of the older houses are remodeled, flanked by ornate columns, the doors painted bright colors. The boutiques—still expensive— also reflect the change. The sexy clothing in the store windows suggests Victoria's Secret meets Scheherazade.

The old homes are still grand; huge sycamore trees, the bark a silver gray, line both sides of the street. Gardening crews work in some of the yards. Barbara, a single mother, who worked first as a teacher, then in marketing for a Long Island company, used to say she was the poorest person in Great Neck. She still rents the same apartment where she raised her two daughters.

Her ex was unreliable both with child support and attention, sometimes attempting to make it up with often inappropriate gestures of good will. Once, Liza came home with an expensive white Calvin Klein pants suit that her father had bought her for her 13th birthday. "Must have fallen off a truck," Barbara said, acid in her voice. Another time, one of the girls came in with bagels, dozens and dozens of them. Barbara noted that what they really needed was "another kind of bread," a reference to the child support her ex hardly ever paid.

I would plead with Barbara not to speak badly about him to the girls. "He's still their father," I would say. "You don't know how much I bite my tongue," she told me. Years later, when I got divorced myself, sometimes railing in front of my daughter against a man who had done me so wrong, I called Barbara to apologize. My tongue would be profusely bleeding, I admitted, if I had to bite it so often.

In true Barbara proactive, rise-to-the-occasion fashion, she has done her own reading about BRCA. She is "totally supportive" in the decisions I have to make, but as much as she says that I must do whatever "you feel comfortable with, Fernie" with regard to the surgeries, I know she does not want me to have the operations in Ames, Iowa. She wants me to come to New York and offers to take care of me if I have the surgeries done here. "I know the doctors in Ames are your friends," she says, "but..."

Barbara wants a gynecological oncologist to perform the oophorectomy, rather than our friend, Tim; she wants me to have a surgeon who does *only* breasts; she wants me to have a plastic surgeon who is experienced with the most state-of-the art breast reconstruction. I should be in New York for all these things. Growing up on Long Island, it can be difficult to believe that the best and the brightest would live anywhere but New York.

Barbara calls a gynecologist friend of hers who talks to me about "just moving my belly right up to create some terrific new boobs." She makes it sound easy, but I have done enough of my own research about these procedures and the complications that might ensue.

I confess to Barbara that I might not have any reconstruction at all. I have thought of that: the simplest, least invasive

Leaving Long Island...and other departures

approach. She tries hard to be supportive, she tells me how she *is* supportive, it is my decision, after all. But I can tell she is beyond shocked. And that she disapproves. A Long Island girl without a manicure. And now without breast reconstruction.

It is not that I'm such a naturalist or so without vanity that I don't care about how my body looks, but I am cautious. Maybe if I were twenty years younger, I would, without thinking, choose surgical reconstruction.

My cousin Linda does not have the BRCA gene, but has had two bouts of breast cancer, five years apart. One of her new breasts is silicone. The other newer breast was created with her belly fat. Linda's mother, my Aunt Gertie, had breast cancer. To not have reconstruction, Linda told me, would always remind her of the cancer, would always make her feel "maimed." Linda said that if I didn't have any reconstruction at all, she believed I would eventually be sorry.

"You know I will *totally* support you in anything you decide," Barbara tells me now. "Totally. Totally." We are sitting in her kitchen, eating deli whitefish salad, salty rolls, fresh berries. She adds: "But have you read anything about this one-step procedure? They can do reconstruction right at the same time you do the mastectomy. One surgery."

It is difficult for Barbara not to tell me what she thinks I should do. I don't mind, actually. People sharing their opinions with me. There are so many choices. *You have to decide for yourself whatever you are comfortable with*, all the women say on the FORCE website. I am not comfortable with anything.

Friday night is a beautiful spring evening. The weather will be good for the reunion tomorrow. Barbara's phone has not stopped ringing. Nothing unusual. Barbara is always near a ringing phone, more than ever this weekend because she is one of the reunion planners.

Barbara always answers a ringing phone. Because every call is important. My senior year in college I lived with her and two other girls, also named Barbara—it was a very popular girls' name then—in an apartment a few miles from campus. Barbara, Barbara, Barbara, and Fern, it said on the door. Barbara—my Barbara—always got to the phone first. She had lots of friends and was in all sorts of school activities, so the call was usually for her anyway. These days I have had arguments with her about answering her cell phone while we are in restaurants. Or while she is driving. But it is one of the pleasures of my life to have unlimited long distance and access to someone (Barbara) who is always there to pick up.

When we were in high school, Barbara called my house almost every night between the hours of six and seven—the time that I was not to receive any calls because it was dinner time, a rule which was only loosely enforced. My parents would look at me, then at each other every time the phone rang. *Barbara.* My father, whose chair was closest to the phone fielded the call. We had a wall phone in the kitchen with a curled wire that could stretch into the next room. My father said, "I'm sorry Barbara, it's dinner time. Fernie is not allowed to take any calls." Then he rolled his eyes as Barbara proceeded to tell him something that was prefaced with: "But Milton, this is *very, very, very* important." Some begging was involved as well. Sometimes my father held the phone away from his ear so I could hear the urgency in her voice.

Eventually, he'd hand over the receiver to me: "Two minutes," he'd warn.

Barbara then hurriedly told me some news that perhaps was very, very, very important to our high school lives: *that John was going to ask Rosemary out but no one know this yet, that she was absolutely sure she failed the geometry test, that Ellen was such a bitch, you can't believe what she said...*

After a few minutes, my father took the phone. It became a standing joke, albeit an affectionate one, that whenever Barbara called, it was for something "very, very, very important."

Barbara and Fern, 1987

I was in Barbara's living room when the phone rang. She looked at the caller ID. "It's Gabi," she said. Our eyes locked across the room. "You pick it up," Barbara said.

Gabi could not possibly know already. She is calling just to tell me to have a great time at the reunion. Still, *Please, please, please* begins as a mantra in my head.

"Hi, sweetheart," I say, trying to sound upbeat.

"Mom?" Gabi's voice is strangled, fraught with emotion. It seems as if she's about to burst out crying. People mix us up on the phone. Like it our not, she has my nasal voice. When I am at her house in Chicago, sometimes my ex calls and I answer. "Hi, Hon," he says, his voice soft and loving. I stop him: "This is Fern." I know the "hon" is not meant for me.

I cannot make out what Gabi is saying. She *is* crying. She cannot even get the words out. Then I hear: *Great News! I don't have it, Mom. I don't have it. I don't have the gene."*

"What?"

"I don't have it. I don't have the BRCA gene."

It is as if—as if, what? Words fail me for the happiness born of relief. The exuberant, extraordinary gratitude of *nothing happened.*

Mothers have known this in the most mundane of circumstances. You are at the beach. You put on sunscreen, straighten the blanket, look into the picnic basket, trying to find the sandwich a child has requested, one without mustard. And when you look up, suddenly, she is not there. You scan the next blanket and the next down the sand and out to the waves. Terror mounts, the air so close and hot; panic rises like bile in your throat. You call. You can hardly say her name aloud for saying it will give the validation that she is missing. Everyone around you is calm. No one is close to fainting the way you are.

They don't know. The lapping waves are black. But before the screaming starts, you see her, the tow-headed toddler digging in the sand in the shadow of the next umbrella. And that is the moment. The moment when everything is exactly the same as it was before. But different. Because your prayer has been answered and you are in that moment, with all your being, grateful. Everything is the same as it was.

"I don't have it, Mom," Gabi says again. "The genetics clinic just called me with the news."

I ask her to explain everything to me. To repeat the conversation, exactly. I am aware of Barbara standing next to me, quiet, as I fall to my knees; sobs escaping from a very deep-down place.

I have fun at the reunion; I have a few glasses of wine and dance; there will be much talk and gossip and laughter and squeals as I see people I have not seen in almost half a century. Are we even recognizable? Some of us are.

Barbara and I walk down to the canteen hall at the Driftwood Day camp. It is out in the country, very dark, lit by lanterns along a dark path. Barbara and I hold on to each other like two old ladies afraid of falling.

There is Sixties rock and roll music coming from the open front of the building. *Doo lang, doo lang, doo lang. He's so Fine. Goin' to make him mine.* The Chiffons were from the Bronx. There is an open bar and a buffet that rivals any Long Island Bar Mitzvah. But everyone is too excited to eat. There is a din of voices, shrieks of laughter. Some faces I know. Fran, who lived down the block on Warren Place, who walked to school with me, who studied so hard and was nervous before every test. The girls I sat with in the high school cafeteria. "From the lunch table to always," Judy wrote in my yearbook.

Carol Kirschbaum verifies that indeed Mr. Colomby did *not* teach our English class when I was absent. "Yes, I remember that he gave us a study hall," Carol says, laughing. Although I was not in "honors" track, I read all the time: Updike, Salinger, then more ambitiously: Dostoyevski, Camus. There must have been a book he wanted to discuss and so waited until I returned.

There are stories that you remember from your childhood that are yours alone, and even though other people may have figured significantly in the events, they do not know this. It is one of these stories that I tell to Richard and his wife. I know him right away, even though he was quite heavy all through high school, he is not now. Cancer. He is doing all right. He lives in Florida. He is so happy to be here at the reunion. And alive.

When I moved to Long Island in the fourth grade, the term had already started. My mother brought me to Mrs. Ziegler's fourth grade class in Carmen Avenue school. The class on Long Island had already covered long division—something I have never learned to do since we hadn't started that unit in P.S. 95. There were moveable desks where two people sat—unlike in the Bronx, where we had wooden desks with inkwells, bolted in rows. "This is our new girl," Mrs. Ziegler said, introducing me to the class. A redhead with a good figure and beautiful clothes, Mrs. Z seemed very glamorous compared to the stern, Irish schoolteachers in P.S. 95. "Now where should we put her?" Mrs. Z said, looking over the class. Silence. There were a number of double desks occupied by only one student. I stood as if on an auction block. All eyes were on me, the new girl.

Suddenly a hand went up in the back of the room. "She can sit by me," a sweet, chubby boy said. He began to clear off a spot next to him where some of his books were.

"Why, thank you, Richard," Mrs. Ziegler said.

I sat next to him, too embarrassed to catch his eye. He tried to teach me long division, but it never took.

I tell him this story that he doesn't recall at all; his wife, I see, is touched at this knowledge of the kind ten-year old boy on Long Island who became her husband.

Steve Rifkin was the kind of boy the girls could always talk to. He married Laura who was a year behind us in school, and she died of breast cancer when she was just in her twenties, now so many years ago. Perhaps she had the BRCA gene. Every year Steve goes back to the cemetery on Long Island where she is buried. In between the laughter and dancing and the joy that fills the room, I get to talk alone with Steve—the nicest boy who became the nicest man. When I get back to Iowa, there is an email from him: *Don't for a minute think I'm not thinking about you. Every day I have you in my thoughts and prayers.*

And so it begins, the summer of my sixty-second year. The smell of lilies of the valley wafts across the porch with every breeze. I have planted zinnias whose buds will soon offer a border of color on the west side of the house. There are grape leaves along the back fence that Joe will parboil, stuff with rice and lamb and roll into *warak enab*, the recipe his mother used to make. "Ah," he says when he eats a special dish that tastes to him like home.

There is a dinner party game we sometimes play. Name the simple, sensual pleasures of everyday: That first sip of strong coffee in the morning. The one, perfect orange hibiscus flower in full bloom. The shiny, perfect swirl of a newly opened jar of peanut butter. *Ah.*

The pre-op is scheduled for this week and Tim will do the oophorectomy on May 26. He was supposed to leave town, but rearranged his schedule to accommodate me. I thank him for the favor, offer to buy him a great bottle of scotch. "I'm doing it for me," Tim says. "So I can finally relax around you."

From: Diana
To: Fern
Subject: Re: Yes!

Fern, I am sitting here crying that your daughter is negative. That is THE best news I have heard in a long time and it gives me hope for my own!

I will be thinking of you and praying that you get through the next few weeks with ease. Believe me, the anticipation of the surgery is worse than the day. I will be anxious to find out how you are doing. Remember your GasX for when you go home!

This weekend I went jet-skiing on the lake. It was so great to be able to enjoy the outdoors and to think of something other than BRCA. Yes, I am back at work. I love my job, and it feels good to be productive again. The kids are ready for summer break.

I am already anticipating my next surgery... June 19th was so far away and now scary close. Again, it will be good to be on the other side of these surgeries. Anyhow, try to enjoy the good drugs they will give you. I have to tell you, the first day I felt like I was at a spa! Good drugs, quiet room, no pain.

Diana

p.s. And, one more thing... you don't have to decide about the reconstruction yet... USE ME! Watch me go through the process and see if it is what you want. You are welcome to come to any appointment or just LOOK anytime you want. I'm not shy!

13

Genetic test results have implications for blood relatives. In consultation with an appropriate healthcare provider, you may wish to discuss sharing your test results with certain blood relatives who may be at risk. If you decide to do this, you should also consider the best way to make this disclosure.

(Informed consent form to reveal genetic history)

My brother did not respond well to the news about our genetic inheritance. That is, he did not respond the way I thought he ought to. Ray might say his response is more clinical, less emotional than mine. I would say he comes to realizations later than I do. I could also say, he's a lawyer, worse, an academic—he *teaches* law. Exchanging information can be like a courtroom interrogation. I called Ray right after I found out the news about the BRCA gene. He asked a lot of questions: *What were the statistics, exactly, and how was the sample taken? How was I sure the lab results were accurate? Shouldn't there be a retest just to make sure? Was I going to go for a second opinion?*

Maybe we are alike in more ways than I'd like to admit and competitive with each other. Ray and I are close, simpatico in many of our responses, but certainly we have felt the intensity of sibling rivalry, the impulse to get under the skin of that one whom you've known the longest. Years before child safety seats, my brother and I bounced like BBs in the back of the family car, taking turns to ride on the shelf atop the rear seats. I teased my brother relentlessly, not giving him a turn, getting into his space, feigning innocence. Finally, Ray hauled off and hit. This infuriated our father. "If I stop this car, you'll both be sorry," Dad would say. There is no one who can quite get to you in the maddening way a sibling does.

Years ago, we were out together with our spouses for dinner—I don't even recall what the conversation was about—but my brother and I got into an argument and we were both insistent on being right. We wouldn't let it go. I was thinking at the time, although I didn't say it aloud: *Boy I could never be married to him.* My brother actually DID say aloud: *Boy, I could never be married to you.* Then he added a flourish: *Fern, you can be such a ball buster.*

When I told Ray that the recommendation of health care professionals in dealing with this cancer mutation was prophylactic surgery he asked, "What does that entail?" I told him that I was going to have my ovaries and fallopian tubes removed. I added: "And I'm I going to have a double mastectomy."

There was silence at the end of the phone. I felt as if I were delivering an unwelcomed package, and he wasn't sure he wanted to open the door to receive it. "Well, you don't have to do anything yet, Fern," he said. "This doesn't seem to be an emergency." I was feeling accused. Of what? Being female and hysterical? In the very next breath, Ray mentioned his children: "I'd like you not to tell Lizzie and Abram. I want to do that myself. If I tell them anything…"

"Of course," I interrupted. Then I added: "But you have to tell them, Ray. You have to let the kids know." His son, Abram, was married and didn't yet have a child. Lizzie lived in California with her partner, Sarah. When Iowa's supreme court affirmed the right for gay people to marry right after Proposition Eight denied this in California, I emailed Liz and asked if she'd like her Aunt Fern to make a wedding in Des Moines. Lizzie worked as a wellness director at a college (she has custodians do hip-hop to stay in shape). She is very creative

Leaving Long Island…and other departures

and fun. Once she sent me a country and western music tape she made entitled: *It's Hard to be a Vegetarian Cowgirl.*

My brother doesn't like being told what to do—certainly not by me, his older sister. Lizzie was going to be thirty and childless. That put her at additional risk for breast cancer. I told Ray that if he did not share the information that I had tested positive for the BRCA1 gene, then I was going to tell Lizzie. She'd want to know. I told Ray: "You have to get tested first. Your insurance will cover it because of mom and me. But BRCA1 is dominant. So if you don't have the gene, the kids won't have to be tested at all."

"I'm going to read about this," he said. "I don't know enough. But it does sound as if you're being alarmist."

I tried to keep an even keel, not let him hook me. "The news is alarming. I'm not making this up, Ray."

Again, there was a long pause. "Well, I have to tell you this: I might not get tested," he said finally. "I'll have to read up about it. I might not do anything at all."

I felt the blood rush to my face. "Put Lynn on," I said, wanting to speak to his more sympathetic wife. I don't remember what I first said to her, but I might have started the conversation by calling her husband an asshole.

Early next morning the phone rang. It was my brother. "Are you calling to apologize?" I asked. "I don't know, let me ask my advisor," he said, trying to be jocular. I heard him yell: "Hey, Lynn, am I calling to apologize?" I heard her say that he was.

I recalled that when our father was first diagnosed with cancer, I went down to Florida and called Ray from the hospital. I had seen the way the doctor looked when he came into the waiting room after Dad's exploratory operation; the doctor's eyes were so sad. Mom—already fighting her own breast cancer—was sitting with dad and I was alone in the waiting room after the doctor left. I called Ray, crying. I knew that the news would be bad—that the cancer, originally in dad's lungs, had spread to the brain. "Ray, I saw the way the doctor looked when he came out..." I began.

"Don't tell me about the look in the doctor's eyes, Fern," my brother said, cutting me off. "What's the prognosis?"

Perhaps Ray was scared. Or responding in that very male way that drives women crazy: *Don't tell me how you feel, we can fix this, what's the prognosis?*

Only a month earlier Dad was playing tennis in the morning, before the Florida sun got too hot. Then he went to work. As a teacher's aide, his second career after the fur business, he had been the oldest person to work in the Florida school system—he retired when he was seventy-eight to care for mom. Our parents, Milton and Ruth had been together for fifty-six years. Mom called dad "Bubbie." He called her "Bubbie. "The Bubbies," my brother and I said when referring to the parental unit. On their last anniversary, I had called: "How's the marriage doing?" I asked. Dad replied without missing a beat: "We're working on it."

Family experts say that the relationships between siblings change after the loss of parents. Brothers and sisters can get closer or become estranged. My brother and I got closer after both the Bubbies were gone. Ray calls frequently and shares the news with me: Lizzie onstage or on the tennis court, a job offer for Abram, all the ramifications of the politics at the university where he works (the only time I actually egg him on to go on the offensive, where I enjoy the stories of the trouble he stirred up against some bureaucratic nonsense. My brother and I do

Fern and brother Ray, 1951

Fern and Ray, 1990

share the same political bent. If we worked together, we'd get along famously.)

A few weeks ago he called to tell me that Lizzie got into grad school at Harvard. "Harvard?" I was amazed. Lizzie is fun, adorable and bright as a button. But Harvard? My brother and I were both laughing our heads off, "Oh my God, Ray. The first thing I thought of was *Legally Blonde.*" "Me, too! Me, too!" he exclaimed. But so happy about Lizzie. Then serious: "We're orphans," he said. "Who else can I brag to now with mom and dad gone? Harvard!"

Eventually—not even eventually—soon after I had told Ray about the BRCA gene, he did get tested. Why couldn't he just go ahead and do it without giving me such a hard time, I wanted to know. I didn't ask him that, though. My mother would say: "You know him, Fernie. That's just the way he is. Just leave him alone. Don't start up with him."

When he called to tell me about his BRCA test, he was crying. There was such relief in his voice. "I tested negative," he said. There was a wait and some confusion because the genetics clinic was supposed to call back. Some mix-up. He was upset about that, but I wasn't really listening to that part. He was negative. Lizzie and Abram would not have to be tested. Negative. "That's great, Ray," I said. But to be honest, there was a part of me that wanted my brother to test positive for the BRCA gene. To be as crazed and worried as I was for his children. After I had hung up the phone, I confessed this dark thought to Joe. "Just my brother, not the kids," I said.

"Oh, honey, you don't really mean that," Joe said, shaking his head.

There are bad men around. My brother is not one of them. He can be trusted. He is faithful to his wife. He is not a

Leaving Long Island...and other departures

bullshit artist. Although Ray would tell anyone (and frequently does) how much he admires me, his big sister, he can get my temperature rising faster than anyone I know. Now I can imagine him reading this. *Oh, come on, Fern, you think it's easy dealing with you?*

14

Fern,

To show that I was raised well, I would like to formally thank you and Joe for the scotch. You have many friends in town. People keep coming up and thanking me for not damaging you in surgery.

(Note from Tim Leeds)

Last year, I was walking home from school when I saw Joe driving down the block. "Hey," I called, flagging him down. He opened the car window, looking pale and strange. "Where *were* you?" he asked, his voice shaky. I was usually home for dinner by 5:30. It might have been 5:45. "I thought you'd be home by now," he said, visibly upset. I knew something was wrong when he pulled over to let me drive. "I think I might pass out," he told me. Chopping up onions for spaghetti sauce, he had lopped off a bit of fingertip. Holding up his left hand, he showed me the blood seeping into a dish towel.

On the way to the hospital, Joe didn't speak except to request that I not take Duff Avenue, a road that often has passing trains which delay a direct route. I concentrated, looking at the cars in front of me, not the hand he had raised above his head to staunch the bleeding.

I parked in the lot abutting the hospital's emergency exit, and we went in together. The emergency room was empty. Two nurses were chatting quietly with each other at the front desk. Soon after, a limping teenager arrived in athletic gear accompanied by two friends. The place exuded calm and did not seem very emergency-ish.

I gave our insurance information, signed a form, and a few stitches later we were home. Joe took a couple of aspirins. I wiped off the bloody kitchen counter, reheated the pot on the stove and made a salad. We were starving—so I didn't look very hard to distinguish blood from the tomatoes. Anyway, it was a very good red sauce.

The hospital in Ames, Iowa is clean and well-run. The personnel is made up of friendly, competent Midwesterners whose only defect is that they can be a tad too cheerful—especially at six in the morning when I was scheduled for admission before the oophorectomy.

I had been waking every morning with a sense of dread. It is a state of mind I remember from when Zachy was a baby, and we had to keep taking him for more tests. In the morning, rising from the reprieve of a deep forgetting sleep, my first thought of the day was always *oh no*. There was something wrong with my baby. I wished what was happening to be a bad dream. *Oh no*—terrible, to have those be the first words that go through your mind upon awakening. And then facing the day with dread because you know what you don't want to face is really happening.

Dread. The long summer of my first marriage blowing apart, I recognized this feeling again. I woke alone. Had I really believed that the marriage I thought was solid and good for so many years was over? I awakened to my new single-state, betrayed and unemployed. Could it really be true?

Dread. *Oh no*, is how I awaken now. Although, being older, the falling asleep is not so very good either. I am going to have the first operation.

Joe and I are in the hospital waiting area and I am handed a beeper, although we are the only ones in the room. We're called—beeped—and before I even get to select a magazine both of us are led down several corridors to the out-patient wing, a place of some familiarity: here I had breast lumps removed, following Zach's birth I had my tubes tied; Joe had a pin taken out of his hip; both of us have had colonoscopies.

What I am about to have—an oophorectomy—seems more serious and perhaps I should have a hospital room, at least for a night, but Tim Leeds assures me that this will be an easy surgery, that there will most likely be no reason to "open you up." He has repeated that phrase, "open you up," in an offhand, somewhat cavalier way.

In very short order I say goodbye to Joe and am wheeled down to a holding place, a long room separated by a white curtain from the other out-patients; suddenly there's Tim in a shower cap and scrubs, looking rakish—*How you doing?*—and before I can answer the drugs begin, drip, drip and I am sooo gone. They are the drugs of laughter and forgetting. The reason women keep having babies is because they do not remember the intensity of the ripping pain. The reason we even schedule that second colonoscopy. Drip, drip, drip, and goodbye. Who's afraid of Virginia Woolf or cancer or even not waking up?

And before I know it, some angel voice is calling, "Fern, Fern." Joe's there in the room behind the curtain, loving and steady. He looks tan though worry lines etch his forehead. "You did great," he says. "Just great!" He is encouraging. Under his shirt is a new gold Saint Joseph medal he has bought. The other one was lost once when the loop broke and it had fallen off his neck. Saint Joseph: patron saint of family and fathers.

The canned broth the nurse offers me is the most delicious thing I have ever eaten. And the jelly on the toast—my God, is it strawberry? How does this jelly so capture the sweetness of summer? Everything tastes divine. The nurses wave goodbye as

I am wheeled out to the lobby. I wave back, as if I am headed for a trip and will miss them all. Bon Voyage. Thank you. Thank you. We are told that the valet will bring our car around to the driveway in front of the hospital. Oh my, a valet! And everyone is so darned nice.

I come home that afternoon—the hours melt by, my bed at home so cool and inviting with its navy blue sheets. I sit at the desk and send out emails; the phone is ringing. Our kids are calling. Friends are calling. I did not have to have a complete hysterectomy; Tim said that the ovaries he took out looked fine and clear. My beautiful, fine clear ovaries that are perfect but unnecessary, and no matter, will now never cause a problem. Never, ever. That same day Tim, who rushed on the pathology report, calls to affirm what he saw. All clear. Verified. Definitive. I do not have ovarian cancer.

I love Tim and Joe and our sunny bedroom and my beautiful clear ovaries: I love our Iowa backyard through the south windows, so green and golden that Dylan Thomas would be moved to poetic ecstasy. Giddy with drugs and delight, I am falling in love with everything.

But the next day I ache and have the low-pelvic cramps associated with bad periods and the Braxton-Hicks contractions before childbirth. It really, really hurts. "Totally normal," Tim says when I call. "I just spent some time rooting around in your insides." I think he enjoys saying phrases like that: "Open you up. Rooting around in your insides." He tells me to buck up, that everything is normal; there is nothing at all to worry about. Take the painkillers.

June. It is our anniversary, Joe's and mine. Nineteen years. A while ago we realized that the only way we would live long enough to celebrate a golden anniversary would be if we added up our married lives. My first marriage of twenty. His of eleven years. And next year we would have twenty. That would make fifty.

But with all the distractions, both of us forgot our anniversary. I was planting impatiens on the north side of the house when Joe comes out of the front door. "Hey, do you know what today is?" Joe asks. He comes to the front stoop and looks at the garden. "Nice."

"Oh, I forgot." I stand up and stretch. There is still another row to put in the ground.

"I forgot, too," he admits. Then: "Do you want to go out for dinner?"

I am in the ripped work-shirt I often wear for gardening chores. Joe already has lamb chops defrosting for the grill. We can go out for dinner any night we want, can't we? The girls are finished with college, and we have enough money; no one left to feed at home; going out for dinner is not such a special occasion any more. "What do you want to do to celebrate?" he asks.

"Happy anniversary," I say, a clump of moist, red flowers still in my hand. I tell him that I am already doing just exactly what I want to do.

15

Rich or poor, it's good to have money.

(My Uncle Morris)

My mother's insurance company had denied her claims for "pain management" when she lived with us in Iowa and before she qualified for hospice. I spoke to a young man from her Florida HMO and tried to describe the pain in my mother's chest following her mastectomy, which, unfortunately should have been "managed" in Florida. I gave up and we ended up paying for the pain clinic ourselves.

I recalled the frustrating phone calls to the insurance company when Gabi was in New York; they refused to pay almost every time Gabi had her blood tested for a thyroid condition because they had "already made payment"—not realizing that although the tests were the same, the dates were different; the exact same tests were required every three months to assure that her thyroid levels were normal. Gabi was in law school then and still on my insurance since she was a student. She had recently been diagnosed with a hyperactive thyroid and the doctors were trying to adjust her medication. There was that last bill before she graduated. I couldn't bear starting from square one to make those calls again to the insurance company. I paid for it myself.

The time of my planned surgeries, I did research about BRCA1, talked to doctors and the insurance company. Along with the stress of having the BRCA gene it was difficult to deal with codes and exceptions; to be put on hold, listening to music I would never be subjected to unless I was stuck in an elevator.

I try to be nice whenever I talk to someone from an insurance company. Both because I know it is not the fault of the person in the cubicle trying to help me, but because I think the person in the cubicle would be more willing to help if I am polite. Really I want to scream into the phone: *If we can pass any substantial health care reform which to my mind would mandate single payer health care, this conversation is over! And so is the bloated salary of the CEO. And no one should even think of striking it rich with a multi-million dollar tort case. That's over, too! And could anyone explain how health care "managed" by conglomerates is saving us money?*

Instead, I say, "Thank you. You have a nice day, too."

About money—well, I've always had enough. It's been my experience in the Midwest that people don't usually ask how much things cost. They feel that money (how much you got), like sex (how much you're getting), is a private concern. It has seemed odd, this delicacy around what is really a material matter. Why should money merit such scrupulous inattention? Yet, after living here for most of my life, some of this has rubbed off.

What is comforting is to have *enough* not to have to scrape by, eke out a living, go from hand to mouth; to have enough not to worry-worry-worry about where the next meal is coming from, how to keep the roof over your head, or make do. It is not, as the song says, having nothing left to lose that makes you free. But having enough not to care so much. Having enough money so that you have time and energy for things other than survival.

When I married in 1968 I fancied myself just hippie enough to reject the white gown, the buffet of chopped liver shaped into a chicken, the photographs in front of the fountain at the Huntington Town House like every other bride in the albums from those Long Island wedding mills. My father asked if I wanted a big wedding or the money a big wedding would cost. It took only a few seconds before I had my hand out. My father signed a check: three thousand dollars. He also said wistfully: "I've always wanted to walk you down the aisle."

So, my husband and I had *enough*. Enough to put a down payment on our house when we moved to Iowa. Then the starting salary for an assistant professor in the philosophy department at Iowa State in 1971 was 10,300 dollars. Originally they had offered 10,000, but my father insisted: *ask your boss to pay for the move.* Joey was embarrassed to negotiate with the chairman of the philosophy department. Maybe he felt it wasn't something that academics did. Also, the early 70s was the start of the glut of Ph.D.s looking for work and the offer at Iowa State was the only job offer he got. I think the way he phrased the request to the chair was: "My father-in-law will be angry if I don't ask..." The chair said they couldn't pay for the move, but as consolation offered the extra 300 dollars a year in salary. Since salary raises are increased on a percentage basis, this decision ultimately was a far better deal for us than had the university paid the flat fee for us to move across the country.

When we bought our house I began graduate school and became pregnant, ultimately having to pay for the C-section and the six days I spent in the local hospital because, when the insurance company counted back, they concluded that the baby was conceived *before* our coverage began. An operation and six days in the hospital cost close to 1,000 dollars in 1972. We took money out of savings and paid it off because we had enough.

Joey and I hardly ever had arguments about money. It was considered *our* money together. If we bought something for the house that cost more than a hundred dollars, we usually talked about it. I think we had the same values about what to spend money on—not that there was ever *that* much of it. Living in a mid-western college town where people didn't signify with clothes and cars and *stuff* helped us not want things we didn't have. We bought books and records; we had baby-sitters and went to the movies; we flew home to see family. When the kids were born, we started college savings accounts. We had enough.

My second husband thought seriously about early retirement when he was just fifty-seven and we were encouraged to make an appointment with a "financial advisor." My friends and I used to have conversations about problems with our kids, our love-lives, the complicating intersections of work and families—well, now we talk about stock, retirement plans, options, buy-outs. It is only recently that I have used the word "annuity" and have discussed with some seriousness how to "protect the assets in our portfolio."

TIAA/CREF is the college teachers' retirement fund. Offhand, I can't recall what the letters stand for, and I've hardly paid attention to the statements over the years. Except the numbers before 2001, when Joe was thinking of taking early retirement, the numbers were big enough to make our jaws drop. All those zeroes were confusing. Funny money. "Can we possibly have this much money?" Joe asked.

We actually have three retirement accounts. My husband's, mine, and the settlement following the divorce from my first marriage. Many years ago, a woman I know got divorced, and I remembered her saying how dumb it was not to have asked for half of her husband's pension. She was too young when the marriage ended to think about pensions and her not-very-good lawyer must not have thought about them either. I believed myself to be securely married at the time that I heard this, but somewhere I stored that information.

My mother bought the house in Plainview in 1956 for 17,500 dollars. She drove out from the Bronx to Long Island with her friend, Chickie, looking at houses as if they were shopping for shoes. They had seen the split-level model of the house on Warren Place. What used to be potato fields became a development of identical tract houses with streets named Deborah Drive and Judith Avenue. Deborah and Judith were daughters of the builder, Sam Hochman. One street was named Hochman Boulevard until the homeowners protested and renamed the street "Shelter Hill Road." Ours was going to be the last house on a dead-end street—the term cul-de-sac was not used then—and ground for the last house, 4 Warren Place—was still unbroken.

My mother put down a fifty-dollar deposit and started planning her kitchen. The original layout, with the stove across the room from the sink, was impractical, she said, designed by a man, most likely, who didn't cook. A stove should be in an L next to the sink. This bit of advice I have carried with me in planning the kitchens of my adult life.

"I bought a house today, Milton," my mother told my father when he came home that night from work. "I bought a nice house in Plainview." This act, her independence and will, very much defined my parents' relationship.

"Plainview?" My father was confused. "You bought a house out in New Jersey?"

My father worked, my mother stayed home with us kids. Every week he'd put her household money on the dresser, sticking out of her jewelry box. There were crisp twenties, I think five of them. Sometimes she'd say she needed more that week, and he'd give it to her. I never thought of her house money as *his* money and I'm sure neither did she. But he was keeper of the accounts.

My father kept extra money in his sock drawer, the second from the top of his dresser. There was usually a roll in one of his black dress socks, an occasional ten or twenty in the argyles. When I was a teenager, I had free access to the drawer, as long as I reported how much I took. I'd say, "Oh, Dad, I went shopping today and bought shoes for $3.99." That's how much the pink ballet flats were at Chandlers one summer.

My parents hardly talked about money, and it was something they didn't seem worried about. This is interesting to me now, since my father had his own business and some years were good years and others were bad. I heard that kind of talk: how business was bad that year, or even a couple of times how the fur business was *dead*, or how the business was all *going to the Greeks*. I had thought that was an expression: like the business was going to the dogs. But literally, Greek people had taken over the fur business from the predominantly Jewish merchants. Still, I never made the connection with money: how much we made that year or how much we had if business was good or bad.

After my family made the move from our Bronx apartment to Long Island, we lived a stable, suburban existence, untouched, it seemed by financial exigencies. We had a cleaning woman and a gardener. My parents took a nice vacation every year. We ate steak and lamb chops each once a week. I had piano lessons, braces, sweater sets. My brother had a closetful of sports equipment. We both went to camp.

When I was in junior high, my friend Harriet's family bought a Cadillac. I was impressed by this when her father pulled the shiny, black car into the driveway. I went home and told my mother that Harriet's family must be really rich because they had a Cadillac. My mother said: "Well, we could have a Cadillac, if we wanted to."

My family always had Fords. My father bought one new and drove it until it wasn't new anymore—usually about eight years—and then bought another, paying in cash. My parents took good care of material things. They hardly ever redecorated and kept their appliances a very long time. They never said "we can't afford it" about anything; only that something "wasn't necessary."

When my mother told me that we could, in fact, afford a Cadillac but didn't *choose* to own one (because a car's purpose was just to be reliable, to get you where you are going, and having a fancy one "wasn't necessary"), I understood something about their attitudes toward money.

But when I was in high school and my mother took me shopping for a prom dress, she let me buy the most expensive one in the store. It was a dress I had fallen totally in love with at first sight: white organdy, strapless, with red roses on a green stem sewed along the bodice. My mother and I were in a small boutique and she had told me to try on any dress I wanted to, without even looking at the price. "You look beautiful," my mother said when I put on that gorgeous gown. "Let's get it!" It was 1964 and the dress was $52.00. "It's only money," my mother said.

The next year, my Uncle Morris, my great-uncle actually, left me a small inheritance when he died. Uncle Morris was a widower who used to take the Long Island Railroad in from the city and sit in the driveway with Papa and smoke cigars. Morris, my grandma Celia's little brother, whom she had brought to America soon after she had married, while the rest of the family remained in Europe, worked with Papa, as a house painter in the city.

In America, Uncle Morris married a bad-tempered woman who, to hear my mother tell it, never cooked him a decent meal and who played cards all the time. "Night and day," my mother used to say. "She died at the card-table," is what my family usually said whenever anyone made reference to Morris' wife. Their only child, Frances, who inherited her mother's susceptibility for gambling and high blood pressure, also died young.

Uncle Morris, early last century

Morris was sweet and had a good sense of humor; like my papa, Morris worked hard and never complained. Alone for the last twenty years of his life, he lived modestly in an apartment on a pension from the Painters' Union. Once, after his first heart attack, he came to convalesce at our house in Plainview and shared a room with Papa. I remember coming home from high school and seeing the two of them sitting on lawn chairs in the driveway. "Fernie," Uncle Morris would call out. "Your mother is opening up an old-age home here on Long Island."

Sometimes Uncle Morris would say to me, "You don't worry. I will take care of you." I didn't know what he meant by this cryptic statement. As a teenager in suburbia, what was I supposed to be worried about? Why would I need to be taken care of? And if anyone was going to take care of me, why would it be my sick, elderly uncle?

But a few years later, when Uncle Morris had a final, fatal heart attack and my parents read the will, they were surprised. Morris had money in the bank. Enough to leave over fifty thousand dollars to charity. I was left $7,500. It seemed like an enormous sum of money.

"You'll give half to your brother," my father said in a tone that revealed this was a non-negotiable decision.

My first reaction was: Why? Uncle Morris wanted *me* to have the money. I had a closer relationship to Papa and Uncle Morris than my little brother. I often made them lunch, talked with them. Ray was running out the door to play ball; he had no use for two old men and their stories about the old country.

I don't remember if I ever got to forcefully voice an objection. "If you don't split the money with your brother, you can just pay for the rest of your own college with it," my father added. Realizing I would come out ahead by giving half of the money to my brother, I agreed.

Leaving Long Island...and other departures

Before Joe took early retirement from the university at only fifty-seven years old, we went to see a financial advisor who worked out of a new business park on the outskirts of Ames in what used to be a cornfield. Almost everything on the outskirts of this town used to be a cornfield. Joe and I waited in an anteroom that smelled like new carpeting and air-conditioning—there was a short story I used to teach in which the phrase "new money" is repeated like a refrain; that's what kept running through my mind.

From the inside office, we could hear voices, a bit of jovial laughter, and when the door opened, who walked out but a colleague in our very own English department. He and his wife looked as pleased and satisfied as if they'd just spent the afternoon having leisurely sex. Seeing each other, we all seem a bit abashed.

Next. It was our first visit with the financial adviser who didn't work for Iowa State, but was an Iowa State alum and seemed to be *the* financial adviser to all the professors. He was described as low-key, but aggressive with regard to actual investments. Taking a cursory look over our papers—our TIAA/CREF from the university, my SEP account from my meager writing income, our certificates of deposit—he nodded encouragingly. Aside from the $45,000 left on the mortgage and a car payment of $258 a month soon ending—we had no outstanding loans.

"Let's see here," he said, spreading everything out on his desk. He was the sort of stolid Midwestern type who inspired the calming confidence you find in fathers on old sit-coms.

"Well, this looks like you're in great shape." I felt proud, as if we were getting a good report from the dentist. "You know," he told us. "You've got enough to retire right now."

For a lump sum we paid to him, there would be three meetings. He would lay out the options, proposing our individualized retirement plan, "If you want to do this now." He told us that some people will choose phased retirement, not because it is financially advantageous, but because they don't feel ready to stop work entirely. "Some people only have work," he said. "They love their work. Some don't have other interests." He described what our options were, talked about reallocation, suggested putting more of my money into growth investments, which, since I was not taking retirement might be the thing to do. He showed us charts and graphs with colored bars and arrows. I glanced at Joe sitting next to me and knew that he was not paying attention. He had heard only that we have enough money right now for him to retire.

At home, I asked whether Joe might feel strange, seeing himself as a retired person rather than as a college teacher. "What will you call yourself?" I asked.

"I'll call myself a retired college teacher."

"You don't think that some of this might be difficult?" It seemed retirement had as much to do with defining yourself as it did with having enough money for the rest of your life.

"Not at all," he said easily. He was standing at the stove, sautéing onions that he slow-cooked until they caramelized into a sweet crispiness. Cooking is one of his "interests."

Joe has little in the way of traditional male ego. I have never seen him play to win with intensity; once I even discovered that he threw in a hand of poker because one of the guys at the bar—who was a regular—wanted to win so bad and Joe had just cleaned up the week before. I have been in his company and witnessed someone holding forth about a topic about which he is actually quite expert—cooking or ancient history or the Bible—still, he would never think of one-upping anyone.

"Retirement. Shouldn't we talk about this seriously?" I asked.

"We are," Joe said, holding his spatula aloft. "We're talking right now. I'm going to retire! You don't have to. You can keep working for the rest of your life." He added, "But if you want to stop working, we do have enough."

We were not as rich as we thought, of course. Everyone who looked at a nest egg saw some of the cracks. Perhaps I was rationalizing when I said that the market boom of the past decade is not particularly good for the American character, for ordinary people to become almost rich by doing nothing at all to earn it. I think it is wrong for our country to have executives make more money leaving a failed corporation than cops and firefighters and teachers make in their lifetimes. We're happy to have seen some of them fail, but aren't those CEOs also the embodiment of the American dream? Of having it all—and then some?

Over sixty, we pay attention as our friends who, with increasing frequency, are "going for tests." A prostate cancer here. A by-pass surgery there. One of the reasons we hesitate to stop our daily work is that maybe we will have too much time on our hands, too much time to think—about an elbow's nagging pain, a change in bowel habits—so that we arrange this last part of our lives around diversions. Golf. Tennis. Bridge. (Note to self: reread *The Death of Ivan Ilyich*). And I suppose it helps to feel needed, to contribute in making the world a better place.

This afternoon, I took a nap in a bed I had just made with new sheets and pillowcases and duvet, 100% cotton with a high thread count. The linens were more expensive than any I had ever bought. "But you're worth it," my cousin had told me, echoing the hair color commercial which justifies an extravagance toward which one might have financial or moral qualms. She is a doctor's wife in Atlanta who has a beautifully decorated home with folk art bought in galleries and a gazebo that overlooks acres of woods. On a recent trip to Atlanta my husband and I had slept in their guest bedroom, and I told my cousin how wonderful the linens felt. We had a talk about thread count. "You spend over a third of your life in bed," she noted with some practicality. "Why shouldn't you feel good?"

Before I fell off to sleep on my new sheets—with the additional luxury of taking an afternoon nap—I finished a magazine article about an American doctor, a Harvard graduate, who runs a health clinic in Haiti that serves the sickest, most impoverished people. Many of his patients die from diseases that could be prevented or cured, if not by attainable drugs then by changes of circumstance: clean water, condoms, food.

There is a disconnect we feel reading the *New York Times Magazine* or *The New Yorker* which has movingly written articles about AIDS in Africa alongside ads for pent-houses in New York and wine-tasting tours among villas in France. Joe and I give money to charity, but I spend on sheets with a high thread count instead of writing a check to a doctor in Haiti doing good work. Then, in defense, I acknowledge that we don't have so much as to be truly ostentatious in the face of global want. High thread-count sheets but no penthouse. Still a lot more than enough.

1964: Impromptu prom picture with mom in her apron and dad in an undershirt!

16

Dr. Taylor is direct and tough. Joe was in the room with me and he actually said to Joe: "How would you feel about being married to a woman without breasts?" It was somewhat shocking, but an important question nonetheless. Joe said, "She'll still be Fern. The same person I married."

From: Fern
To: Diana
Subject: Re: checking in

Hi Diana,

Thanks for writing. I meant to get back to you. Physically, I'm feeling pretty good. I've been gardening when rain lets up and have my energy back. Emotionally, it's still up and down, though not the roller coaster before the oophorectomy. I sleep really well with Ambien, but haven't taken it the last two nights. Don't want to end up a drug addict from this thing. But before I was up a lot in the night, with really awful dreams. Ecchh. And how old do you have to be before you stop having the dream that you can't find the room to take a final exam for a course you never took? Will I be having this same dream when I am in a nursing home?

I have to keep talking positively: Gabi doesn't have the gene, I'm doing something proactive, blah, blah, blah; then reality kicks in and I think—shit, I'm going to have my breasts taken off.

I'm thinking of having the mastectomies at the end of August, so I'd have my summer—especially since I made the decision not to teach in the Fall—I go back and forth about this one? I had told Gabi that I would babysit in July when she goes to a wedding and I want to do it.

Last night one of the doctors Joe plays poker with (John, a pediatrician) came over for a drink, sat with Joe on the porch and I was talking with him about the surgery. John said if it were his wife (that's always my lead-in: what would you do if I were your wife?) he would have it done here in Ames. He said Mark Taylor was not a touchy-feely doctor but he is a terrific surgeon. John had gone with Dr. Taylor to Guatemala as a volunteer in a very poor area and watched him do a lot of surgery. John was very impressed!

You're all done with school now, so that's a relief, but sometimes having time on your hands is not such a good thing. I'm free—if you want to meet for a walk, go to campus town and have brunch at Stomping Grounds. Call or email me if you want to get together before your surgery.

Fern

From: Diana
To: Fern
Subject: Checking in

Fern,

My mastectomies are set for June 19th, less than two weeks away! So now the nerves set in again. I was refusing to take the Ambien too, until Dr. Leeds told me, "Diana, just take the darn drug." So, I am taking it and figure that is one battle I don't have the strength to fight right now because I need my sleep in order to process all of the rest of this. I am cutting it in half though, 5 mg.

Thanks for forwarding that information on Dr. Taylor, it all helps to calm me down. I am less than two weeks out. Just sent my reconstruction consent in today. That was emotional—I just couldn't believe that I was consenting for someone to cut off my healthy breasts.

I have to be around during the mornings to be a taxi for baseball and softball. However, I would love to get together any day this week after 2 pm if it works for you. I just want to be with someone who "gets it." I'd be happy to meet you for a walk, go to a park, anything, just be with someone who doesn't make me feel like I'm crazy!

I envy you in that you have such a personal contact with all of these doctors. I'd like to have them to call each day to reassure me. If you can talk Dr. Taylor into letting you in the room, you can come watch!!

Diana

From: Fern
To: Diana
Subject: You're not crazy

Hi Diana,

Thanks for the offer to let me watch Mark Taylor. But I think if I did, I'd be on the next plane to anywhere. When I had my second C-section in 1976, they had just started giving locals and the doctor asked if I wanted to watch. I said, no thank you, just wake me when it's over!

I feel that sometimes I am consumed by this and am a burden on Joe (though he never makes me feel as if I am). Since I have found out about the BRCA I have not gotten undressed for bed without thinking of myself getting undressed with a scarred, breastless chest. Would I still get undressed in front of Joe? I think if we don't face these things then we'll really get crazy later on.

Fern

From: Diana
To: Fern
Subject: Support

Fern,

Jim and Joe probably need to form a support group! I know that this process is difficult on them too. However, Jim continues to be my rock and refuses to show his fears. We are blessed to have supportive men.

I am struggling with confiding these feelings with my closest friends. I just took them through this whole emotional process a couple of months ago with my last surgery. It feels selfish to be bringing them along with me again. They all did so many favors for me and listened to all of my anxieties. I just feel like it is so much to ask. They are all busy/exhausted raising families.

When you see Mark Taylor on Tuesday please remind him to be extra good with me when he operates on me. I want him to KNOW who I am!

One summer, I started calling Margarita Mix my "friend." This summer I have a new friend named Ambien. One summer at a time. Have to tell you—the Margarita Mix was a whole lot more fun!

Diana

From: Fern
To: Diana
Subject: Re: Dr. Taylor

Hi Diana,

Joe and I saw Mark Taylor today. You know that we've seen him socially a couple of times, that Joe plays poker with him—but really I don't "know" him the way I know Tim Leeds. Taylor answered every question, made me feel good about having this surgery here in Ames. He is very confident as a surgeon. But he was also honest talking about possible complications.

I asked about going to a surgeon who "only does breasts," and would that be a better choice. I asked how many breast surgeries he does. Over 70 mastectomies a year, he told me. He knew the studies that showed "both sides" of the issues—about how many same surgeries a doctor does compared with outcomes. He said that he performs "many more complicated surgeries" than mastectomies. As in "that's a good thing"—he's not just a breast-remover machine. I asked him when he would recommend that someone see a "specialist," and he rattled off a number of operations where he would—but not a prophylactic mastectomy. I asked him if he would be comfortable having Allison (his wife) having this done here in Ames. He said, "Absolutely."

One of the things that impressed me the most was that he went on the FORCE website. I had told him about it. We talked a lot about how much information is good, but you have to be wary.

He assumed that I was going to have reconstruction. Everyone does. He asked which plastic surgeon I chose from Des Moines. I told him I wasn't sure yet that I would do reconstruction, and I think he was taken aback.

But then he was supportive, said there were sometimes more complications with reconstruction. I am not saying this to scare you—you are making the right choice.

Joe would be a help. There are drains and some disgusting stuff, but he is not squeamish and very good with his hands, with small motor skills. He was always in charge of untangling jewelry chains, taking out splinters, etc. He was a single dad for seven years and is quite adept with vomit, body fluids, etc. But I think he was glad to have married me before the girls got their periods. Teaching them how to put in a tampon was a bit beyond him.

I also talked to Dr. Taylor about "waiting"—since I could have the time off in the fall, medical leave with pay and I just really don't want to have another operation so soon. After the oophorectomy am feeling really good right now. I'd like to get back into exercising and into shape. Well, whatever shape I was in.

Dr. Taylor said waiting this short time would be a responsible choice. But he also said that if I changed my mind, that I chose to do the operation sooner, he could do it with less notice. I asked him if that was a bad sign, that he wasn't all so booked up in advance. He smiled at that one.

When he examined me he said that I have fairly "young" breasts. I guess that means they weren't down to my knees. Apparently I also have good muscle in the chest wall with not much fat and no "rolls" under my arm. That seemed to impress him as a good thing—surgery-wise.

And yes, I talked about you and said I knew he was doing your surgery on Friday. He asked how I knew you and I said that Tim Leeds introduced us. I told him that you wanted him to know who you were "as a person." He said, "Oh, I know who she is."

What does that mean? Maybe Tim warned him?

I feel the fragility of the physical body. I was looking at my pinky finger last night before I went to sleep and it was twitching and I thought "Parkinson's disease."

Fern

From: Diana
To: Fern
Subject: Re: Dr. Taylor

Fern,

I am glad your visit went well with Dr. Taylor. I guess I'm not sure if it is good that he knew who I was or not!? Funny... Leeds said to Taylor, "Before you can be Dr. Boobs for the stars you first have to 'pass' Diana and Fern!" At least we have them on their toes!

I am spending the day trying to get everything in order here. One of the hardest parts about going into surgery is that we are so VERY busy with kids at this time in our lives. I am lucky to be home with the kids in the summer but, as we live in the country, I am a full time taxi driver. I want my kids' lives to go on as normal, to notice my surgery as little as possible, so I am trying to think of every angle of their schedules. I just want them to be KIDS! This topic is not something they should have to think about too much at their ages.

My mom (really my step-mom, but she raised us and I think of her as my mom) and dad will be coming tomorrow night to help out. So, I am trying to get the house in top shape so that my parents can focus on the kids. I also ordered several meals to be made and put in the freezer from a place in town that does that. It will be nice to have my mom around because she is a great caregiver. This is all a bit harder on my father than we realize. I think my situation reminds him of all he went through with my mother that eventually led to her death. He was supposed to be on a fishing trip to Canada with some guys this week but cancelled to be here. So, I will keep him busy with ballgames, etc.

Jim knows my need to control. He told me that I would do the surgery myself if I could!!
Diana

From: Fern
To: Diana
Subject: Re: Advice

Hi Diana,

Yes, it is good that Dr. Taylor "knows who you are." But John (our pediatrician friend) said that Taylor would treat me the same as he would a poor peasant woman in Guatemala whom he was never going to see again.

You're talking about worrying about everyone else, your dad's feelings, your kids. But you can let them take care of you. Sometimes "taking" is also a gift to those who are the givers—it makes children feel good to be useful in a crisis. I always thought that Joe did too much for the girls and didn't let them do enough for him.

Ok—enough "advice." Meanwhile, I am also a person who usually cleans my house and has everything in perfect order—even if we drive to Des Moines to go out to dinner. In case, there's an *accident, I don't want a sticky kitchen counter or dishes in the sink!*

There's nothing I kept from you about what Taylor said about the mastectomy. I thought 70 operations a year was a good number because it seemed like enough practice. The reconstruction does make the recovery more difficult, but there are so many women who are pleased with the result. If I were your age, with your athletic life, I would do the reconstruction without a second thought. Friends I speak with seem surprised that I am considering not to have reconstruction. I feel mixed. But I suppose if I am bereft without breasts, I can do something later on.

This is going to be all right. And you won't get cancer and will be there to dance at your daughter's wedding!

I was reading Joe your email about planning for all activities of the kids, your dad, ordering meals to freeze, etc and he said: "Couldn't she do something about the conflict in the Middle East?"
Fern

From: Diana
To: Fern
Subject: Re: Advice

Hi Fern, Tell Joe I'm busy Friday, but I'll get to work on the Middle East first thing Saturday morning! It is good to be needed.
Diana

Afternoon, June 19
Email from Jim Elliott

Jim,

After surgery, hit the reply all button and email this group of people. To those receiving this, please feel free to pass Jim's message on to people that I missed. Thanks for all of your love/friendship/support...

Please pray for me, my family and friends, my doctors/nurses, and my new friend Krista that is also BRCA 1+ and having this same surgery done today in Chicago.

Time to get this day going!

Diana

17

"Pray for me," Diana said. I wish I could. I would like to believe that a gentle and good higher power had some influence.

Diana had given me directions, but it's easy to get lost on country roads in Iowa. One wrong turn and it seems as if there's cornfields forever. Diana's post office address was Story City, a town just north of Ames, but in fact, she and Jim were out on an acreage; I went past the house, already down the road when I realized that I had passed the marker. Packed in a picnic basket in the back seat was a fruit flognard that Joe had made. The car smelled like warm peaches.

The house was huge, gleaming and modern on a tract of lawn in the middle of open farmland. When I first moved to Plainview, there were still farms surrounding our suburban houses. We children played in empty lots in fields that once grew potatoes. We'd jump into holes dug for new foundations, play hide-and-go-seek behind dark mounds of dirt. Perhaps the chemicals used in those fields were one of the causes for the high rates of breast cancer on Long Island.

Diana came to the door, dressed in white shorts and a shirt with buttons up the front. I handed her the dessert. It looked pretty, decorated with berries and mint from the garden, Joe's artistic touch. "Wow. Fancier than we're used to," she said. She looked fresh and pretty, too. Jim had helped her wash her hair, she said. I held back from a hug and carefully patted her on the back. She was trying not to take any more pain medication because it made her sick to her stomach, but the Tylenol just didn't do much. "I'm choosing pain over nausea," she said. She had more range of motion than she thought, though still unable to lift her arms higher than her shoulders. "I can't open doors." She gave a little smirk. "Guess I won't be escaping anytime soon. "

Everything looked new and clean in her home, the furniture man-sized and comfortable. Outside the big picture window we could see fields and trees along the horizon, the clear, blue sky. There were hay bales across her front lawn, neatly packaged bale after bale. "It's so beautiful here. So relaxing. No wonder you love living in the country," I said. It looked like a painting by Monet. Or was that Manet? I always got them mixed up. Diana had a drive to the middle school where she taught. Not so relaxing in winter on two lane roads covered in snow.

"Want to have a look?" Standing by the window, Diana opened her shirt. There were small mounds with plum-colored bruises along her chest wall. "Things are starting to pucker up as the swelling goes down," she said. Two V-shaped incisions were on either side of her chest; drains had emptied into a pocket of a camisole made specifically for mastectomy operations, taking away "all the yucky stuff." She couldn't wait to take the drains out, All the women on the FORCE website said this. How disgusting the drains were. But if the drains were removed too soon, the fluid could back up, and they would just have to be put in again.

"Oh, Sweetie," I said, witness to this assault on her perfect, little body. Beyond the established camaraderie of our medical situations, I felt real affection for Diana. She was funny and smart and generous. I told her that after all of this was over, Joe and I would have a dinner party with her and Jim, Leeds, Taylor and their wives. Everyone who, as Ruthie has said—had seen our "private parts."

"What would we talk about?" Diana said, smiling. "Not religion. Not politics. Not sports." She knew enough about how our interests and opinions differed on so many things. She added: "And we'll be so sick of talking about BRCA."

Diana was religious, a committed Christian. While I believed my genetics was the result of random happenstance, she envisioned a purpose, a design greater than we could imagine. I am envious of those who have faith in contrast to my undemanding and tepid agnosticism.

During the first few years of Zachariah's life, when we kept going back and forth to the hospital in Iowa City for tests and more tests, I did a little make-shift praying, making deals with a god I didn't believe was there. *If Zach would only by all right, I would... whatever.* There were many promises. I would devote my life to a good cause, adopt an orphan, abandon my selfish, bourgeois life. Crying in the bathtub, I submerged myself in a desperate, bargaining baptism. *If Zach could only be normal, if he could miraculously begin to walk and talk; if Zach would only be all right in the end, I would promise to*—to what? Spread God's word? Become an orthodox Jew? *And where have you been all this time,* God might ask.

When Zach was still a baby, my beautiful, difficult mother-in-law was very sick. Muriel had been in pain for months, but stubbornly refused to go to a doctor. "What for?" she challenged. "So he can tell me that I have 'the big C?'" She continued to smoke unfiltered Pall Mall cigarettes.

Muriel was fifty-six years old when she died of stomach cancer. A grandma then to both Gabi and Zachariah. But fifty-six, an age that seems to me now so unreasonably young.

We were in Plainview that summer. My own mother, in an attempt to offer solace or reason when there was none, kept asking: "What's it all about?" She repeated this often enough that the phrase ended up as part of the familial *shtick* of my first marriage. "What's it all about?" Joey and I used to ask in response to the tragically inexplicable.

As a little girl, I once asked my mother about heaven. "Nope, not there," she said, always the straight shooter. This could be a little harsh sometimes. When I was four years old, my mother told me that the Santa I saw in the shopping center was just some guy dressed in a red suit and fake beard, hired by Macy's. The tooth fairy? "It's daddy who puts the money under your pillow." While my mother was not good at creating magical moments, there was something reassuring to know that my mother was forthright. Is the shot from the doctor going to hurt? "Yes, but then it's over very quickly."

Mom had a notepad by the phone. It was one of those complimentary gifts that you get in the mail from a charity asking for a donation. This pad had printed across the top: *The Truth From Ruth*. Totally fitting.

What happens when we die?" I asked when I was eight or nine, feeling alone with deep thoughts.

"Well, you didn't know anything before you were born. And that's the way it's going to be after you're gone," she said matter-of-factly.

"Where would I *be* then?" I asked.

"You wouldn't *be*," my mother said. "But it doesn't matter, because you wouldn't know it. You wouldn't be there."

I imagined myself no longer "there," everyday life going on without me. It was chilling. I remember conjuring up the physical feeling of "not there" in an assembly at school, feeling so much older and wiser than my classmates. Boys with cowlicks. Chubby girls in plaid jumpers and Buster Brown shoes. Innocents, all. The music teacher blowing on her pitch pipe to begin. Then all of them blithely singing "God Bless America." Me, *not there.*

There are more moments now, in this winding down time of life, that questions come back unanswered. Often in a panicked stab when I put my book on the night table and turn off the light before sleep. How it would be with me not there? And *what's it all about?*

What does an agnostic do but focus with intensity and purpose on her own life's gifts and the world of wonder. If not the hereafter, then the here-and-now: The smell of the cedar mulch as I spread it in the flowerbed. The faithful man next to me in bed. From the skylight above us, a summer night of stars.

College Graduation, 1968

Fern

Barbara from Plainview

Barbara from Flushing

Barbara from Corona

18

Time has come today,
The young hearts go their way
I don't care what others say
I have no place to stay...

(The Chambers Brothers)

"Oh, your step-mom used to be really pretty," said one of Katie's friends, looking through an old photograph album. There I am with a sweet smile, pearls around my neck, my hair in a perfect flip; then in college, blond bangs, straightened with gel and tape, full-lips, like a pouty girl out of a French film. I am the exact same person today. Except different.

As a teenager, Katie would try on pair after pair of jeans when we shopped together, me waiting outside the dressing room, refolding all of the rejections. "Do you think I look fat in these jeans? How does my butt look in these?" she would ask modeling every pair. Good, good, good, I said. She rolled her eyes, never quite believing me. There is a point in every mother's life when you just become worn away, willing to spend an exorbitant amount, all the grocery money, anything, on a pair of jeans that might make a teen-age daughter smile when she looked in the mirror. Once, clearly exasperated, I told Katie to forget about her ass and just work on her personality. She has brought that one up to me on more than one occasion.

This July, a much more confident Katie will be thirty years old, the cut-off that people my age were warned about. Do Not Trust Anyone Over Thirty. Which was said by someone who probably didn't get paid when the phrase was used on posters put up on dormitory walls. In college we listened to

The Chambers Brothers: *The Time Has Come Today*, the longest, most remarkable song consisting of rhyming doggerel. The pulse was relentless. Then a cow bell became slower and slower, stopping time, before it picked up again. I remember listening to this song, sitting cross-legged on the floor of our college apartment, sharing a joint, eating brownies and potato chips.

I remember sitting on the floor, cross-legged in P.S. 95 for kindergarten story-time, looking at my knees, flexing and watching as they changed shape from shiny knobs, then examining the soft fold of flesh that formed in the inner side when I bent my leg. That skin looks the same today. The backs of my hands, the pouches under the jaw, the skin along my neck—not so much.

These memories are mine, but how can they be fact-checked? Aren't the memories of our young lives revised and reconstructed? I can call Barbara and ask her if she remembers sitting on the floor of the Sherbrook Apartments in Cortland, New York with the other two Barbaras, getting stoned and listening to the Chamber Brothers. But there is no one, no witnesses who can verify that five-year old girl, bored in an over-crowded kindergarten class, looking at her knees. In telling our own stories, the memories are selective and few, we embellish and forget.

Now in my sixties, I stand on one leg, then the other, while I brush my teeth for the longest two minutes in the world, the time the electric toothbrush takes to finish the cycle. I read in the AARP bulletin of this multi-task exercise to maintain balance.

The body. This home of skin and bones, a structure that holds up for a long time, but eventually becomes no longer dependable. My brother Ray can't jump or shoot or run the way he used to, even with his new hip. As a woman is it more difficult to accept aging if you had been accustomed to men looking as you walked by? I suppose there is a certain freedom in my invisible, older self.

Once, driving with my mother along Old Country Road, we stopped at a light, then waited, even after it turned green, as an ancient man made his way across the street. "He was once a little baby and his mother used to kiss his feet," my mother said as we watched him slowly trudge up to the curb.

I was the one who used to cut my grandfather's toenails after his bath. In the winter, Papa wore long underwear under his clothes, even in our warm house, where the thermostat was kept at seventy-two degrees. My grandfather's baths, maybe a monthly occurrence, involved a shave, the trimming of hair, a second set of clean long underwear set out on his bed. After the bath, flushed and red-faced, Papa would sit on a kitchen chair, newspaper spread before him; I sat on the floor with a large nail clipper and an emery board. Papa was tall and thin and had elegant, long feet, but each yellowed, gnarled nail was thick and ridged as corduroy. I cut carefully, then filed along each nail to make it smooth. I liked taking care of Papa in this way, although I was not always compliant in my service.

I didn't say, "Do I have to?" when my mother had asked, but I must have felt some resentment for having to come home from high school and miss lunch with my friends those few weeks of my senior year in high school. Papa had taken a fall on his way to the candy store to buy his cigar. He didn't break any bones, but badly bruised the side of his face and was unable to wear his false teeth. He became more confused than ever. For a while, he wouldn't eat, unless someone fed him. My mother was working full-time then, and so my job was to come home for lunch, heat up the jars of baby food that she had bought, and feed him lunch. There was a disgusting array of canned meats mixed with vegetables. Papa liked the sweet potatoes and squash. Each glass jar made a satisfying little pop when it was opened.

I snapped open one of the jars without even reading the label. They all had the same picture of a round-faced Gerber baby with rose-bud lips in a surprised pucker. One jar was Liver and Bacon. I paused for a moment. None of my grandparents ate pork, although all the next generations did. Papa was in his mid-eighties then, but no meat from a pig had ever crossed his lips. I had already opened the jar, scooped the contents into a pan and put it on the stove to warm.

"This is delicious," Papa said, after the first spoonful. He opened his mouth for more. "Babies eat this?" he asked. "This is delicious, Fernie." He repeated in amazement: "Babies eat this?"

I never told my mother, but she wouldn't have thought it was anything terrible. My father's side kept Kosher, but she thought dietary restrictions were silly superstitions. I felt vaguely guilty. But Papa enjoyed that lunch so much. And eighty years is certainly a long time to have never tasted bacon.

I write this now, thinking how intimate I was with the body of my grandfather, and then my parents at the end of their lives. I helped my father when he could barely walk and stood beside him as he went to the toilet, both of us embarrassed, but I was afraid to let him get up from the bed to go to the bathroom by himself. I tried to act nonchalant, official even.

"Let's go, Dad." I said briskly. "Stop talking to me like you're the nurse," he told me.

Mom came and lived with us in Iowa after Dad was gone, but then decided she wanted to go back to Florida. I had heated discussions with my brother about how much care mom actually needed. For one, I was adamant about her not driving. Mom told me that she only did a few errands, going to the grocery store, to the doctor. She assured me that she "only made right hand turns." She drove very slowly—like many of Florida's elderly drivers—but she was also somewhat addled. One woman in her condominium had driven her car into the lake at Covered Bridge condominium. I could see mom doing that.

On one visit down to Florida I talked to mom about giving up driving. The condo had a bus that took the residents grocery shopping or to the mall. Also, mom had lots of friends who were still competent drivers. "I'm going to talk with her about taking the car keys," I told my brother. We could leave the car in Florida for when we came down, but I was afraid if I left the keys, she would still drive. Ray countered my suggestion. "You're so controlling, Fern. Why don't you just lock mom into the apartment?" When I spoke with mom, she was a whole lot more agreeable. "You're right, Fernie," she sighed. "I shouldn't be driving any more."

When her cancer returned I convinced her to come to Iowa and live with Joe and me. She read in the chair by the south window of our bedroom on the first floor and still raided the chocolate jar. But within weeks we ordered a hospital bed for the spare room and arranged for Hospice. My mother had lost speech in the last week of her life. Giving my mother a bed-bath alongside the hospice nurse, I stood at the foot of the bed, rubbing cream on her feet, massaging each toe. The hospice nurse gently washed mom's face with a warm washcloth. "You are lucky," the nurse said to my mother. "You have a wonderful daughter."

My mother managed to raise her chin and smile from the pillow, her blue eyes lit with love. Something palpable passed between us. "Wonderful!" My mother mouthed the word, though no sound came out. My father had died the year before. I knew that, very soon, I would no longer be anyone's daughter.

In July, a few weeks before I had decided to schedule the mastectomies, Joe and I went to Chicago to babysit for Wilson and Ruthie. Wilson was already over two years old. There was little interest in toilet training but a lot in balls, machinery, vehicles. All the attention we give to non-sexist childrearing, but some of this must surely be hard-wired.

It was on that trip that Joe's back gave out after the six-hour drive from Ames. We were tense with so much Chicago traffic that last hour coming into the city. And we hadn't stopped enough to stretch as we always say we should. Both of us have had back problems on occasion. There is nothing like that instant when your back goes out to make you feel the body's vulnerability.

Gabi and Bill were leaving for a wedding on the East coast; in an attempt at diversion, Joe had taken Wilson for a walk down the block where city workers in hard-hats were fixing the street. Wilson, always in motion, could sit calmly, transfixed at a construction site. He didn't know his alphabet, but he was able to clearly distinguish a cherry picker, a dump-truck, a utility van. In the car, he yelled with excitement: "Big digger, big digger, big digger"—and the family all feigned enthusiasm. Once Ruthie said: "I hate to tell you, Wilson, but I don't like trucks. Mom doesn't like trucks. Dad doesn't even like trucks." Nonplussed, he called out again: "Big digger!"

Gabi and Bill live in the city near Lincoln Square on a block of older homes with stoops, front porches, the houses all quite close together with garages and alleys in the back. The street in front of their house is one-way with speed bumps, so although they are right off a busy commercial street, there is a real old-neighborhood-feel of kids playing outside; all the families know each other. There are probably thirty children on the block and—because women have babies later these days—a few sets of twins.

Joe and Wilson were sitting on a neighbor's front stoop; they sat and watched for a long time. Then, reaching down to pick up Wilson (who, of course, wasn't ready to leave), Joe felt a lightning stab of pain in his lower back. He was pale, in a sweat, by the time he came back to the house. "I don't know how I made it," he told me, while I searched the cabinets for painkillers.

Joe spent the rest of the day on the floor. "I'm sorry," he said, unable to help with dinner or even able to sit up for a children's good-night story. Wilson, in his semi-terrible-twos, was not especially cooperative in heading upstairs for a bath or leaving the bathtub once he was happily playing in it. "You be careful of your back. Don't lift him," Joe warned me. "Oh, what a time for my back to go out."

"Honey, it'll be all right," I said, taking a fresh ice pack out of the freezer. Joe asked me to search the suitcase to find the book he was reading.

"I'm sorry," he said again, needing my assistance to rearrange the pillows he had set out on the floor. "It just hurts so much when I move."

"Don't move. I'm here," I said. I was already dreading the ride back to Iowa. We have defined roles. Joe shops and cooks. He knows how things should work around the house and how to fix them when they do not. I clean, do the wash, pay the bills, make social arrangements, call the children. He drives in traffic. This is the balance of a marriage. And when one is down, the other rises up. In sickness and in health. There was joking sometimes about some of our friends' parents. One could see to drive. The other could hear. One could walk. The other could remember. Together they made a complete person.

When we got back to Iowa, I went to the cancer clinic and met Mary Ellen to try on a prosthesis. Joe was with me and she invited him into the dressing room. Turning to me, she asked: "Is that all right with you?"

I supposed it was. Maybe this was part of the counseling protocol, to involve the husband in the process. Sort of like when he's a "coach" and offering ice chips when you're in labor, screaming in pain and really hating him.

Joe watched as I was fitted with a white sports bra, a beige, lacy bra, and a white bra with thick straps. The prosthesis itself, inserted in the pocket of each cup, was flesh-colored. Well, the color of my flesh. There must be fake breasts made in tans and darkest browns. These were soft and squooshy, made of a gel-like material which did feel exactly like real breasts. There was even a ridge that slightly defined a nipple. I held a breast in each hand, testing them, like I was about to juggle. The pair together was heavy. A couple of pounds probably. It would be hot wearing this in summer.

I am easily uncomfortable, preferring flat shoes, loose clothing. Like my mother. She sold real estate on Long Island when the market was really booming in the early Sixties. There were these dresses she wore—Wilroy knits—straight sheaths that showed off her figure. High heels. Nylons attached with garters to her girdle. Mom would come home from work, already unzipping as she walked up the stairs from the garage. By then, I had set the table for dinner and made the salad. She went right to the bedroom, took off her stockings and unpeeled the girdle. Her housecoats were pink and feminine.

I was in high school when my mother and I both got contact lenses—the hard kind. Much as we hated our eyeglasses, neither of us could adjust to the lenses. Mom couldn't even wear Tampax. "I feel it in there," she used to say. The Jewish princess and the pea.

Which was why I hesitated so about having reconstruction. It wasn't only the more complicated medical procedures that made me nervous, it was the idea of having something "in there," that I would not be able to take off if I were uncomfortable.

Are the Chambers Brothers really brothers? I just posed the question to Google. Yes, four brothers from Mississippi who played in their Baptist church: Joe and Willie on guitar, Lester on harmonica, George on washtub bass. *The Time Has Come Today.* The song was so long, more than ten minutes. But it seemed as if time really did stop when we were listening to it in college. There were over six hundred comments about the song, even in the last few weeks. My favorite: *Aw, is it over already?*

19

"Here? Or here? What's the difference?"

(Cornell University, 1965: a boy at a ZBT fraternity party, touching my shoulder then my breast, to justify his copping a feel)

Everyone smoked cigarettes in college. In the dorms. In the cafeteria. The apartment I shared with the three Barbaras was always filled with smoke, the big glass window in our living room smogged over with a hazy film. I was mostly a social smoker, at parties, and never had a cigarette before lunch. Barbara—our Italian roommate from Corona—was hard-core. There was a cigarette dangling from her mouth first thing every morning, before she made the coffee. She smoked Salem Menthols, which no one else liked, so we never grubbed cigarettes from her. *Salem. Salem. Don't inhale 'em*, people used to say. In the apartment the ashtrays were always full.

We smoked even in the classrooms. One of the first things a professor would do before a lecture was light up. That gave those in the class a signal to begin. Just as it was impolite to begin eating before your host sat down and lifted the fork to her mouth, it was considered bad manners to light a cigarette before your professor. We carried these little ashtrays, the ones that looked like origami folded to tell a fortune. In the winter, with the windows closed, the air in the classrooms would be blue with smoke. Everyone—even the non-smokers—must have stunk in those days. The Greek houses permanently had the acrid smell of stale cigarettes and beer.

In college, I was in awe of how some of the girls could really drink. On Friday afternoon, the girls in my dorm would walk downtown to The Tavern or The Hollywood, order pitchers and then stay out for hours. Kathleen and some of the other Irish girls on our floor, could leave after class on Friday afternoon and then stay out until curfew. Not an experienced drinker myself, I nursed a glass of beer for a long time. I used to go back to the dorm and take a nap, a shower and eat dinner before heading out to a party. Years later, a man I knew said: "In college, I used to like dating the Jewish girls. They could never hold their liquor and then I could take advantage."

Sometimes I took a chartered bus to Cornell with my Barbara's sorority, Sigma Rho Sigma, which she had pledged freshman year. While I went with her to rush—the teas before induction—I decided at the last minute not to join any sorority. We were moving apart then. Barbara was all school spirit and had a boyfriend on the football team. I was listening to Bob Dylan and wearing black turtlenecks. I went to poetry readings and drank the cheap Chianti that tinted everyone's teeth red.

Politics made us take sides, too. I remember going to hear the Black Activist Dick Gregory speak in the student union against racism and the war in Vietnam. He was so inspiring. I was cheering along with the crowd until there was a line about armed revolution, about taking a gun and going to the suburbs. I stopped and thought, *hey, my parents are in the suburbs.*

Rho Sigma—Sig Rho—had a reputation of having the most attractive and smartest girls. Gloria with her dark eyes and prematurely silver hair. Sandy Benjamin, a beauty queen with her blonde hair in a sophisticated French knot. For solidarity, the Sig Rho sisters wrote their letters and took class notes in purple ink. The Violets.

The day that the sorority acceptance lists came out was rainy and miserable; I was loathe to leave the comfy dorm room to go up the hill to the student union and see the postings. It was all quite secretive. You had to give your identification to a registrar; no one else could find out for you.

Barbara, Barbara, Barbara and Fern (Cortland, 1968)

"Just come with me to see if you made Sig Rho," Barbara pleaded. That was her sorority of choice. "Even if you don't want to join, don't you want to find out?" She added: "You might decide to join."

If the weather were better, I might have gone that day. But by then I was adamant in my refusal to join *any* sorority. There were the stereotypes then of sorority girls—junior leaguers, superficial, material girls. Everything that I didn't want to identify with in the 60s, though in retrospect, the idea of a sisterhood has its appeal. I am sorry that my prejudices caused me to have missed that experience.

I shook my head. "Besides, I made Sig Rho," I said.

"How do you know?" Barbara asked.

"I just know," I said, further infuriating Barbara with my arrogance. I really thought I did, too.

Cornell University was Ivy League with a plethora of smart boys and a shortage of females. We would ride the half hour to Ithaca, primping, reapplying lipstick as we pulled up into the driveway of a grand fraternity house: Sigma Alpha Mu (Sammy, the Jewish fraternity), Theta Chi, Zeta Beta Tau. ZBT—which we used to call Zillions Billions Trillions, supposedly was the rich boy fraternity. The boys waited outside as we exited the bus, looking us over. I remember stepping off the bus with Barbara and hearing someone say: "Wow, all these girls are pretty!"

In the party room of a fraternity basement, a boy whose face I would not be able to recall to pick out of a line-up even the next morning, grabbed my hand and claimed his stake for dance after dance. He brought me a drink called Purple Passion, vodka with grape juice. The basement was hot after a while, all those steamy bodies, the dank odor of spilled beer on upholstery and the cloying smell of perfume and hair spray. The drink in a plastic tumbler was cold and delicious; I couldn't even taste any alcohol. But when I got up again to dance, I felt funny. "Whoa," I said, clutching his shoulder for support. He led me to a chair, sat down first, and pulled me onto his lap. He began kissing me, touching me, along my back, then my breasts. I was rebuffing him in the most half-hearted way, turning my head away, moving his hands away from my body as if in slow motion. "Don't. I'm dizzy," I confessed, as the room began to spin. "Let's go to my room for a while, so you can lie down," the boy suggested tenderly. He took my hand, leading me up the stairs. "Wait," I said.

Somehow, instead, I made my way to a bathroom on the main floor and over to a sink, where I splashed cold water on my face and looked long and hard at the girl in the mirror. I willed myself not to throw up.

I stayed long enough in the bathroom, so that the boy began to send in emissaries, inquiring about my condition. First: was I all right? Did I need help. Then: when was I coming out? There was a chair in the bathroom, and I sat down, surveying the traffic. Doors, slamming, streams hitting the bowl, sighs, flush, washing of hands; girls at the mirror sat on the ledge of the sink, smoking, reapplying lipstick.

Again, I could hear the boy asking about me. I don't think he knew my name. Suddenly, I became quite calm. I looked at the bathroom window. Too small to crawl out of. But I would just stay there in the bathroom, safe, until I felt like myself again. Until the bus came to take us back to our college dorm. There was the chair which looked so cozy. I should have brought a book with me.

I don't remember what happened after sobriety kicked in. Maybe the boy finally gave up and left, searching for some drunker, more compliant girl. I knew that I had just dodged a bullet. There wasn't even a name for it—what happened to so many drunk young women at fraternity parties, at mixers in 1965. Date rape.

I've been thinking about breasts, looking at breasts of women I pass in the street, dreaming of breasts. My own had arrived so late. In sixth grade, everyone seemed to be getting breasts and I had nothing, not even the little buds that popped like ju-jubes on adolescent chests. There were those girls who developed too early like Shelley Moskowitz, who in elementary school had boobs, cinched waists and the hips of a real woman. Men turned as they walked by and sometimes called out dirty things. She was trapped in a grown-up body when others were still playing with dolls.

I was always grown up in my head. I knew things about sex. I read Photoplay movie magazines from my cousins and knew veiled secrets concerning the sex lives of the stars: infidelities, botched abortions, over-doses. I still looked like a little girl.

Too early, too late, a girl is always self-conscious. I wanted to be a real teenager. At fourteen I could still get into movies for under twelve. In the mirror, my chest was flat as a skillet. Breasts appeared eventually and by then I was just grateful.

In junior high, I stuffed a bra, 32 AA with the cut ends of nylon stockings. I wore a tight cardigan sweater buttoned up the back, a black scarf, pulled tight and tied around the nape of my neck. White lipstick and dark eye-liner. When I walked out of the house, my father would ask: "Where you going? To the corner to meet Angelo?"

In high school, when my breasts were small and fit with the rest of my petite frame, the bras I wore were lightly padded. Sometimes boys would sneeze when a big-breasted girl walked by. "Achoo! I must be allergic to foam rubber," a boy would say, much to the amusement of his friends. But the small-breasted girls like me—who were really padded—the boys didn't have a clue.

One college summer I had bigger breasts. This was because I was on birth control pills, the ones that had just come out with probably enough estrogen to create a human Barbie. Which is what I looked like that summer, except in miniature. I had real breasts. They didn't seem real. They bobbed like water balloons, floating atop a narrow torso. I got whistled at that summer. On the beach, roughhousing boys would suddenly tumble on to my blanket. When I stopped taking the pills, my breasts deflated within weeks.

Most of my life, I didn't have enough to need a bra, and good thing, because the women's movement said it was fine if you didn't wear one, and bras annoyed me anyway. They always rode up. I was happy not to have to wear one. But many big-bosomed women who were identified as feminist and free must have been made uncomfortable by pendulous, unsupported breasts.

I knew a girl who said that she had an orgasm when her boyfriend touched her breasts. Once she even had one fully clothed, in a movie theater. "How does he do it?" her friends asked, thinking it was because of a special technique on his part. We would have liked to show our boyfriends a trick or two. The question should have been, "How did she do it?" She said it wasn't him. She was super sensitive "there."

Megan, my older stepdaughter is in the bedroom on the computer, when I am getting undressed to take a shower. The girls and I are not modest with each other; many conversations have taken place when someone is putting on make-up, someone is peeing. With three girls in the house, Joe was

Megan, Joe, and Katie, 1997

relieved when they went away to school, so he didn't always have to have his bathrobe handy when he left the bedroom. Now Megan is living in an apartment in town, working in a daycare center. She comes over frequently for dinner. "Could I see your breasts?" Megan asks, turning from the computer screen. "Sure, I guess," I say. I pull my tee shirt over my head and stand, facing her. Megan must have seen me undressed before, but now she pays attention because I am going to have a double mastectomy. "You have really nice breasts," she says. "They're hardly saggy at all."

"Well, thanks, I guess. "

"Are you going to miss them?" she asks.

"I don't really know," I say.

In the shower, I look down at my breasts. True, they aren't saggy, but lower on my chest than when I was young and used to go bra-less in summer tank tops; there are faint scars on

Leaving Long Island...and other departures

my left breast from the biopsies, but no stretch marks; there are some hairs around the nipples that showed up after each pregnancy. Soaping up, I cup a handful of each breast. More than a handful is wasted, isn't that what the men of small-breasted women like to say? With two soapy hands, I part each breast along the line of cleavage, making them disappear. Goodbye. How will the chest look flat again?

20

Some things I did not do so far in my retirement:

- *Play golf or tennis*
- *Pet animals at the local shelter*
- *Tutor refugees*
- *Volunteer at a food bank*
- *Read to the blind*
- *Deliver Meals on Wheels to shut-ins*
- *Become a Big Sister to a troubled teenager*
- *Teach in the prisons*

I am not against doing any of these things (except maybe golf), but I cannot boast, as many do, "how busy I am" in retirement. Even though I read all the time, clean my own house and have organized our bills, medical records and receipts into colored folders, I am decidedly *not* busy. I read the morning paper carefully, making politically astute comments to Joe, who is only trying to finish the crossword puzzle. I peruse the obituaries, noting how many of the newly departed are nearer our age than not. The newspapers no longer mandate *cause of death* which sometimes spikes my interest, reading between the lines to hypothesize about suicide or AIDS. I take long baths, go out for lunch with my still-working friends and then come home for a nap. I watch *House Hunters,* my new television show of choice on HGTV. I cannot believe how entitled young people are when disparaging a master bedroom that is deemed too small or a 70's kitchen that new buyers insist would simply *have* to be remodeled. I was happy as a twenty-something in my first house in Iowa, though the only bathroom was so tiny that the toilet, the sink, the tub were all within a foot of each other. It was less than half the square footage of the house on Long Island— and way older. There was a sagging back porch, no dishwasher of washer/dryer, a tilted kitchen floor and a boxy refrigerator I had only seen in old movies. It was a first house. I was happy there. Now when I drive by this little Dutch Colonial, only a few blocks away, it seems even smaller. I was a young married there. I am a newly retired person now in a brick ranch with a Jacuzzi tub and a master suite.

Someone told me that the best thing about retirement was that she was able to drink a leisurely second cup of coffee in the morning and read the newspaper. But as a university professor, I have always been able to do that since I never had a class that started before 9:30. It was a great job, although leaving did not anguish me, so relieved was I never to have to grade another student paper.

In my retirement I have exercised on the treadmill in the basement and plan on making this a habit. I have eaten leftover fettucini alfredo at four in the afternoon (I hope not to make this a habit). Everyone applauds energetic old people with verve and nerve who are still trying everything new under the sun, retirees who say that they just don't have enough hours in the day. I find the length of the days sufficient. It's the years that are managing to slip-slide away.

I can legitimately say that *I'm writing* when people ask how I am keeping busy in retirement. There seems to be a hint of apology now about this enterprise. Like a woman at home who is not bringing in a paycheck: I'm just a housewife. *I'm just doing a little writing.* When I had children living at home and a full-time job, I wrote towards deadline in a more focused and deliberate way. Now other deadlines are drawing near. Both the decisions about the mastectomies and the, oh yes, the more significant deadline, which looms ominously. I am trying to say this without seeming maudlin or unnecessarily gloomy. But at a certain stage of one's life it seems appropriate to plant fast-growing shrubs when making landscaping decisions. Our enormous, old Butternut tree was felled in the last storm. It was the largest of its kind in town, the tree guy told us as he suited up with a safety belt and began the ascent, a chain saw over one shoulder. I was sad to see the tree go, but also relieved: During severe weather I feared that a limb would crash through our bedroom skylight. After the tree was down we could see the rotted inner center of the stump. "Trees die, just like people," the tree guy said.

There is the evaluating of one's life while putting off both panic and regret. Should I have joined the Peace Corps right out of college instead of accepting that job teaching junior high school in upstate New York where my new husband was attending graduate school? Joey and I had both applied to the Peace Corps right before we married in 1968. This was

First house in Ames, Iowa.
We paid $21,300 for this home in 1971.

a way to avoid the draft and keep him out of Vietnam. We filled out all the forms, and I got recommendations from my college teachers attesting to my maturity and intelligence. Still, I had such qualms. Bugs and other assorted vermin, for one. Also there was the awareness that I was a twenty-one year old English major who did not speak a second language, who grew up in the suburbs in a home with dependable electricity and central heating—not to mention three bathrooms. What could I possibly offer to subsistence farmers and grown women with their too-many children? There was something arrogant about my privileged American self-offering aid.

One favorite English professor was encouraging when I expressed these doubts. Joey and I were young, we had no debts and no ties to keep us from doing something as adventurous as the Peace Corps. My teacher said—perhaps a bit wistfully thinking of his own settled, family life—that there "would never be another chance like this." We should join up, he told us.

Joey and I started the paperwork and would be assigned to Kenya following physicals, orientation and language training, before I bailed out. Joey—a Boy Scout for many years who still fancied himself a good camper and maker of fires—was probably relieved not to have had to schlep me along to Africa.

A sympathetic, anti-war psychiatrist vouched that Joey was unstable—which, in retrospect was probably true. I always suspected that if Joey were ever sent to fight in Vietnam, he would be the first to take the hill and eventually be sent home in a body bag. At any rate, following a number of physicals and a high lottery number, he was not drafted.

Instead of the war or the Peace Corps, we set up an apartment with posters, candles and Indian bedspreads and that first summer of our marriage traveled to Europe. Young Americans were walking around with *Frommer's Europe on Five Dollars a Day* under their arms. You could really do five dollars a day in 1968, eating street food and staying in cheap hotels with bathrooms in the hall. We peed in the bidets.

We met a Jewish Canadian couple, Rae and Jack, who ended up travelling with us for most of the time. Rae was beautiful, with golden curls past her shoulders and a voice like an angel. She had brought a guitar with her from Montreal and had a small Canadian flag attached to her backpack. I felt more confident travelling with Rae and Jack, wanting to pass as a Canadian since everyone in Europe then seemed angry at Americans and our involvement in Vietnam. Also, Rae and Jack spoke fluent French and Yiddish (which helped when we were in towns in Switzerland where German was spoken). She was the daughter of a woman who was a Holocaust survivor. We sat on park benches in Paris and Rae sang *Suzanne takes you down to the place by the river...* lyrics that never failed to bring tears to my eyes. People strolling by stopped to listen. There was a mournful air about Rae that made her singing all the more heartbreaking.

We rented a car in London and drove to Scotland and over to Wales; I was terrified as Joey drove wildly through the roundabouts on the left side of the road. It was cold in the summer in the Scottish countryside. The four of us stayed in a trailer that had no heat, and mice in the oven. I felt proud for braving it out and not complaining. Perhaps I would have been Peace Corps material after all. Rae managed to make a chicken curry with orange juice, honey and mustard, a recipe that I have made to this day for pot-lucks in Iowa. Rae and Jack, young, hippie adventurers, wanted to hitchhike through the rest of Europe. Eventually, to travel to India.

I don't regret not joining the Peace Corps. Or travelling to exotic places. No Regrets. That was the title of my second novel, based on a cross-country trip in a Volkswagen camper that, in real life, I made with an Iowan friend who was leaving her husband for another man. That was over thirty years ago. I thought she was making a mistake. After the book came out, she never spoke to me again. "It's fiction," I told her. Every writer loses a few friends in this work.

Can I regret my bad genes and a long marriage to an untrustworthy man? No. I had Gabi, and a second partner who is my soul-mate. I'll have my breasts taken off and I won't get cancer. Zachariah remains a tiny star of pain and some beauty. I regret not being with him when he passed; but not him. His existence has made me a better person than I could ever hope to be.

A smaller regret is one following the deaths of my parents. Simply that I didn't ask enough questions.

Joe observes my pre-hospital frenzy. I go from one thing to another in a random way, a morning spent digging up begonias and replanting them in a shadier spot; cleaning under the refrigerator; then, still in my gardening clothes, reorganizing the bookshelf and going through Joe's closet. If there is a shirt I don't like, it is left in the basement after I do the wash. Following a significant amount of time, if the shirt is not missed, I put it in the pile with stuff that's going to Goodwill. Joe would never go through my closet. He would never, ever think of giving away something that is mine. Before we go out I inspect his shirt for stains. "You have to change," I say. He looks down at his belly surprised at the grease spot I have pointed out. "How did that get there?" he asks. Before we go out, Joe always looks at me and says: "You look nice, hon."

There's a saying in Arabic that Joe learned from his Mom: *You start cutting hair, you end up pulling teeth.* This describes my random and ferocious getting ready before the upcoming operation; Joe is thinking of things to do to take my mind off it. Yesterday we went to the Art Museum in Des Moines to see an exhibit from an artist, Tara Donovan, who constructs things out of everyday objects: drinking straws, buttons, Scotch tape. I am usually not enthusiastic about this kind of work which often seems silly and more like a class exercise than art.

After graduate school in Chicago, Katie, our youngest, was a curator at a museum of contemporary art for a few years before she went to Austin to get a Ph.D. in art history. I try not to piss Katie off by making critical comments about her chosen field. A few years ago Joe and I had gone to meet Katie in Marfa, Texas, where she had an internship. Artist Donald Judd's giant steel cubes littered the barren Texas landscape. Walking through a field near the artist's compound, Joe barely avoided a pile expelled by some quite large animal. "Watch out," Katie warned. She did not smile when Joe asked if the mound were a part of the exhibit.

In an empty warehouse, strings of colored lights were strung on lines like a haphazard Christmas display. Katie interpreted this artistic expression for the tour. *Anyone could do that*, I thought, but didn't say so aloud.

My mother used to drag my dad to museums and he would say, "Hey, I could do that," when he looked at rectangles and squiggly lines. "Oh, Milton," my mother would sigh. She dragged him to foreign movies, to museums, to lectures. He went along uncomplainingly, making asides. "I could do that," he'd say.

I recall in Mr. Colomby's English class, we read a poem by Carl Sandburg—the one about fog creeping up on little cat feet. A girl in the class said, "Hey, I could have written that." And Johnny Pierson, who looked a little hoody, with tight jeans and a carefully combed duck tail, replied, "Yeah, but you *didn't*."

I love the Art museum in Des Moines, in a building that is cool and filled with light. It is just large enough to walk through in an afternoon without being overwhelming; there's a lovely restaurant for lunch and also an amazing modernist collection in little nooks behind white walls where you can get up close and alone with the art. Iowans don't brag about the collections as much as they should, but then, Iowans don't seem to brag at all. I'm surprised by how wonderful the Des Moines art museum is each time I go.

We saw Donavan's site-specific installation—which I think meant that it was created for a certain place and space and time. Then dismantled and gone. I didn't expect that this display would be so poignant and moving, that paper clips and tape assembled with pain-staking and meticulous precision could become breathing, other-worldly moonscapes or seascapes; that Styrofoam cups could become fields of clouds, like eternity.

21

A woman I know was diagnosed with breast cancer when her husband was on a grant doing research in Europe. "Do you want me to come home now?" he asked when she called and told him about the news. "You don't have to," she said. He came. But she has never forgiven him for asking.

August in Iowa. It always seemed a time of dog-day heat and getting ready for school. Now I will not be working this Fall. I look toward to the beginning of the week, the operation is Monday, acknowledging that this is the fate I have chosen: getting tested for the BRCA gene in the first place, doing the research, having the oophorectomy, now the prophylactic double mastectomy. I am less afraid than I might be before this surgery, because the operation will be "simple" without any reconstruction. Ultimately this is not so much a decision on my part—to not have reconstruction—as it is finally a lack of one, never having made an appointment with a plastic surgeon to discuss the possibilities.

Joe said:
It's up to you, Honey. I just want you to be healthy.

Gabi said:
I'm so proud of you, Mom.

My cousin Linda said:
I think you will be sorry.

Barbara said:
It's totally your decision. Totally. Totally. But did you do all the reading about that one-step procedure?

Diana said:
Look at me. Then you can decide later.

Jeanne, my Iowa-born neighbor, said:
Of course you wouldn't want to do that.

Katie said:
Now you can just work on your personality.

After four months—it seems like years, it seems like days—living with options and uncertainty, I just want this to be over. Joe keeps asking what I want for dinner as if it's a last meal. Finally, he decides on *mjedderah*, a Lebanese lentil dish with coriander and cumin and caramelized onions, which can keep in the fridge when we have company during the week. Also *mjedderah* can be eaten at room temperature atop of a bed of greens and the luscious Iowa tomatoes of August which all of our home-gardening friends have brought over. Tim treats us to dessert and drinks at Maude's. We have wine and crème brûlée and Bananas Foster Flambé. All weekend I eat enthusiastically, although I wonder whether spicy and rich fare is wise before an operation. Perhaps I should spend this final weekend on a fruit juice fast.

Barbara calls on Friday, asking if I received her package. She has the FedEx confirmation number and has traced that the package is indeed in Iowa. "No, sweetie, I haven't gotten anything," I tell her. I add that I hadn't been home in the afternoon, so perhaps a delivery came. But there wasn't any notice on the porch.

"I'm very, very, very upset," Barbara says. "I want you to have this before you go into the hospital." She will not tell me what she sent.

"Will it keep?" I ask. A nightgown for me to wear in place of the hospital gown? Something delicious and perishable? She won't say, but reveals—whatever it is—this gift took a long time to put together which she did all by herself, ruining her nails.

"Something you had to put together?" I can't imagine. Barbara is not exactly the crafty, handy type.

"Well, you'll see." She has some calls to make and will get back to me. "You will love it." She adds: "I'm coming to Iowa after Gabi and Katie leave. I already have the ticket, so I don't want to even hear anything about this."

"Barbara..." I begin. Mostly I'm thinking of Joe. On Sunday night we will drive to the airport to pick up Gabi. Then Katie is coming in from Austin. Then Barbara. It's seems excessive for everyone to fly in from around the country. I don't even have cancer.

"Joe doesn't have to cook for me. I don't need any entertaining. We can just sit on the porch and read. I'll be in the background," Barbara assures me.

"As if you are ever in the background," I tell her.

That night, as Joe and I are starting to watch the news, the phone rings and a woman who says she is from FedEx asks for me by name. "Do you have a friend Barbara on Long Island?" she asks.

"Yes...," I say hesitantly.

"I'm calling you about a package she has sent," the woman says. Barbara has somehow managed to impress a sympathetic FedEx worker with the urgency of a request that her best childhood friend in Iowa receive a gift before she is to undergo surgery on Monday morning. Did Barbara imply that perhaps I might not regain consciousness after the anesthesia? It is not inconceivable. The FedEx warehouse in Ames is closed this time on Friday night, but there would be someone available there to receive me if I could come right now. The woman gives me a number to call to arrange the pick-up. "And good luck on Monday," she says, knowing at least some of the details of the ensuing surgery. She adds that she will be praying for me.

I make the call. I have been instructed by a different woman in the Ames office to "go around to the West door" and knock loudly. People in Iowa always give directions as if everyone knows East and West no matter where they are. Even inside a building. "I'll be right over," I say.

"That Barbara," Joe says as he drives us to the FedEx office which is not far out of town, along the old Lincoln Highway where there is a one-story building next to a Coca-Cola truck plant. I have never been here before. There are (of course) corn fields along either side of the highway, but all the factories are deserted now. Joe and I approach the parking lot which is very, very dark—as is the entire FedEx building— except for one doorway with a glass panel. I knock loudly and a woman peeks through the blinds, eying me suspiciously. I feel as if I should have a secret password.

"Fern?" she says cautiously through the glass.

"Yes." It must be a little creepy working through the night out here by herself. The woman is middle-aged, dark, heavy-set, wearing jeans and a t-shirt. She does not let us in, but opens the door just enough to let me sign something and to drag out a box, a few feet long and quite heavy. "This is from your friend, Barbara," she tells me in a hushed voice.

I think perhaps she is not permitted to do this under FedEx employee regulations. "This is so nice of you," I tell her, profuse in my thanks. "How often do you do this? Open up for someone to pick up a package this time of night?" I ask.

The woman shakes her head. "Never," she tells me.

Joe lifts the package and puts it in the trunk of our Camry. At home, he takes out his Swiss army knife and makes a sharp cut along the side of the package. We are in the kitchen with scissors and lots of assorted knives, but Joe likes to use his Swiss army knife at any opportunity. This is perhaps the third or fourth one he has owned. Others have been taken from his key-chain at various airport check-ins. He rips the tape along the top of the box, but whatever is in there is too heavy and securely wrapped to easily lift out. He cuts cleanly along the entire side of the box and begins slitting open the bubble-wrap.

"It looks like a picture frame," he says, carefully extracting the contents. "Three of them, connected." Fine, wires hang from a thin, silver rod from which hang three separate framed photographs. These seem suspended somehow in the middle of the frame, so the effect of the triptych is one of lightness. On the back of each frame is a block that attaches each photo and makes it seem as if it is floating behind the glass. No wonder Barbara ruined a manicure setting this up.

The photograph on one side is of our daughters: Liza with her dark, Israeli beauty, black curls, beaded, dangling earrings, an arm around Gabi whose ash-blond hair is pulled back in a pony-tail. In the photo on the other end are the granddaughters, Remi and Ruthie, a photo taken the summer before on a visit to Long Island. Heads tilted towards each other, both girls are eating huge slices of watermelon; you can almost see the juice running down their happy faces. The picture of Barbara and me, the middle one of the triptych, must have been taken at the Plainview High School Reunion last May—we are wearing the blue string IDs around our necks. I have not seen this photo before. Barbara and I are hugging tight, we both have hoop earrings and our smiles are wide, showing our extensive dental restorations. Here we are: Barbara and I, friends forever, and the next generations.

Triptych

In Iowa, talk about the weather is never small talk. Weather here is as unpredictable as the people are stable. We take our thunderstorms seriously, watching the sky for the strange, pale hue that presages a tornado. Fierce winds fell trees and torrents of rain can suddenly blind the highway driver.

Gabi was flying in on Sunday evening, although I had told her not to. "You don't have to come," I said. Maybe not that emphatically. Fifteen years before, my own mother had told me not to fly down to Florida when she had her mastectomy.

"Don't come," she had said. "It's ridiculous, Fernie. Daddy is here to take care of me. You're busy. You don't need to come."

A few days later, after her operation, I sat with my father in the hospital waiting room and listened as the surgeon told us that the cancer was in three of the lymph nodes, but he was confident that he had gotten it all. My father's eyes welled up with tears, but it was me who asked the questions about hormone receptors and follow-up chemo. I was almost fifty years old but it was the first time in my life that I envisioned my dad as not the one who was in charge.

Afterward, my father and I went to the deli near their condo and had pastrami and chopped liver sandwiches. He was quiet, as usual. I took on my mother's role to keep the conversation going. Dad still made his old joke when the waitress came with the check. "She'll take it," he said, motioning to me across the table. When I reached, he grabbed it away. Then serious: "I'm glad you came, Fernie," he told me.

Sunday is jungle-hot and humid, but by the time Joe and Megan and I leave for the Des Moines Airport, strong winds and riotous rains begin. Drenched motorcyclists take cover beneath an overpass. Trucks come barreling up behind us. "Put on your hazards," I tell Joe. He is going very slowly and some cars are whooshing by. He is patient with me. Barbara drives too fast. Joe drives too slowly. I have always been a scaredy cat driver, especially when it comes to stormy weather. In my twenties, I totaled a car on a slippery highway, going back to school in upstate New York. "Which way to turn the wheel?" I had wondered, strangely calm as the car began to slide across the side of the road, into a guardrail. Were you supposed to turn into the skid or against the skid? The car flipped over and totally turned itself around; the rail sliced into the dashboard. Sometimes now, in dreams, I imagine myself driving a car without brakes, ice begins to collect on the windshield, blocking all visibility; the car speeds ahead, veering out of control.

The rain stops as suddenly as it began and there's a rainbow, an actual rainbow in the sky over Des Moines. The roof of the state capitol glints gold in the light. We drive down Fleur Drive, landscaped with bursts of end-of-summer purples and reds, prairie grasses along the divides. Short-term airport parking has plenty of spaces, so we all go in. The plane is on time. Gabi comes down the escalator with a small overnight bag—she borrows my clothes when she's here. I wave and burst with pride. My love. She is wearing khaki capris and a plain, black tee shirt and looks like a high school girl home from summer camp. Soon Gabi will be forty years old. On my fortieth birthday, my father sent me a check for a thousand dollars. On a scrap piece of paper, he had written: "For forty years, only *naches*." That is the Yiddish word for joy. For Jewish parents, *naches* sometimes means a particular kind of joy, defined by achievement. As in the *naches* that a parent derives from having a child who gets all A's, is the lead in the school play, becomes a doctor. The *naches* that I gave my father was better because it derived from just being me.

"Want to go somewhere for a bite?" Joe asks, when we get back into the car. We are all hungry, so the four of us eat out, an early supper, in Des Moines. We decide on A Dong's, an inexpensive

Vietnamese restaurant with hundreds of delicious entrees, all numbered and seemingly memorized by the waiters. Des Moines has a large South-East Asian immigrant population, because of Robert Ray, the compassionate Republican governor Iowa had in the 70's. Boat people became Iowans whose children spoke with the flat accent of the Midwest. I have a beer and my fill of scallion pancakes and pot-stickers before the cutoff time. I'm not supposed to eat anything past seven o'clock.

We drive back to Ames, and Joe goes off to watch TV while Megan, Gabi and I sit on the bed and talk until late. Bill and the kids call to make sure Gabi has gotten in all right. Ruthie has been asking so many questions about Gabi's trip to Ames. She had wanted to come, too. My granddaughter listens, listens hard to all adult conversation, the original little pitcher with big ears, and, even at six, has a woman's intuition. Ruthie knows what is going on, attuned, even if Gabi and I have been covert in our telephone conversations. *What? What are you talking about?* Ruthie asks. Gabi has told her that grandma has a bad gene that could make her sick and is going to do some things to stop prevent that. *Sick how? Cancer?* Ruthie knows the word. But Grandma doesn't have cancer. *What things? What things will Grandma do?* Ruthie knows Gabi is upset, has seen her crying and so is on high alert. She has overheard Gabi talking to me about having a mastectomy. How do you explain so a child will understand what a prophylactic mastectomy is? Ruthie had asked: *If Grandma has her breasts taken off, will Papa Joe still want to be married to her?*

Megan has work tomorrow at the day care. I am supposed to be at the hospital tomorrow morning at some ungodly hour to check in. I know the drill. "You don't have to go with us in the morning," I tell Gabi. "Sleep in, and Joe can come back and get you later in the morning. "

"I'm going with you," Gabi declares firmly. "Are you all packed?"

"Packed?" The idea had not occurred to me.

"Mom, you're not going in to have your teeth cleaned," Gabi says. With some efficiency, she starts assembling my toothbrush, a nightgown, the *People* magazine she bought at the airport.

"I'm glad you came," I tell her.

22

To: *Fern*
Subject: *Thank You*
From: *Diana*

Thank you for being a part of my life. I am sorry that we have to share this, but I am lucky to have you. I am thinking of you!

Your upcoming surgery date, August 10th, was my grandmother's birthday, the mother of my mother who passed. Grandma died about three years ago now. So, I will always remember your surgery date. My surgery date, June 19th, was my parents' anniversary so my date will be easy to remember too. We will celebrate these dates in years to come!

For many years Joe has kept a journal, more properly called a log, since there are only the facts recorded, rather than the reflections of his inner life. He takes note of the weather, what we ate for dinner, which friends we saw on the weekend. Making the best of the obsessive compulsive side of his personality, he has maintained a meticulous transcript of the movies we saw, the books he has read, even how long he walked on the treadmill. I asked if he recorded the times we had sex. He said he did, right under his weight for the day, but I shouldn't be "worried," since he put it down in some sort of code. I told him that I wasn't worried that the companionable sex of our older, married selves be revealed to someone who came upon his log. At this point, we are only grateful that this event remains a statistic that can be dependably recorded.

Joe never misses a day to write down the facts of the previous day, going to his study first thing in the morning before he starts the coffee. I used to poke fun at the necessity of his devotion to this activity. I told him: "Yes. This will be good if we're ever accused of a cold case murder." *No, your honor. We were not in Ames, Iowa on the evening in question, July 15th, 1999. We were buying beige towels at TJ Maxx in Des Moines; we ate dinner at the Chinese Buffet and then saw the movie Eyes Wide Shut. Yes, your honor, it was another disappointing Kubrick movie. We both found it silly and pretentious. All those whips...*

These days we consult the log fairly often. Did we make the pork roast the last time Jeanne and Jim came to dinner? How long exactly did Megan live with us before she moved out to be with the new boyfriend? What time of day was it that our granddaughter Ruthie was born? What month was it that my friend Lee died?

On August 10th, 2009, Joe recorded: "Up at 5 to take Fern to the hospital for the double mastectomy." Then, not following the usual log protocol of emotional detachment he added: "She smiled so brave and so scared when Gabi and I watched as she was wheeled away down the hall. This broke my heart."

Joe's log mentioned that Tim came into the surgery waiting room with bagels and cream cheese; that Megan got out of work early and came to the hospital; that all the poker docs stopped by; that my ex came to the hospital and stayed in the waiting room for a while. ("Daddy just wanted to spend some time with you," I said to Gabi, days later, when I had all my faculties. "No, Mom, he was worried," she said earnestly. "He cares about you.")

The first thing I remember is waking up in a sunny room hooked up to an IV drip with Joe and Gabi on either sides of the bed. My chest was bandaged tight, but there was no pain. I drifted in and out the rest of the day. There were flowers on the windowsill. Someone had sent flowers. No flowers, I told my friends. I love flowers, but arrangements are a waste of money, and they always seem to have these depressing little touches—plastic hearts, pink ribbons, cards with generic messages to get well. Most everyone followed my instructions. "These are pretty," Gabi said, in defense.

The first day passed in a morphine fog, dreaming of beaches and sky. I told her that she didn't have to, but Gabi was insistent on staying the night. "That's why I flew in, Mom," she told me. A nurse brought in a folding cot and some blankets. I was high and also a little excited. When your daughter is married and grown with a family of her own, you don't ever get the opportunity to spend the night together, just the two of you. A double mastectomy makes this possible. A pajama party. I can sometimes look at the bright side of the experience.

"Oh, mom, we should have brought the sheep nightgown," Gabi said after unpacking my robe. "Do you still have it?"

"I do," I told her. "It's in the back of the closet somewhere." But I was connected to an IV, and, without being able to lift my arms, the nightgown probably would not have gone easily over my head." I still wear it sometimes," I said.

Gabi was sixteen when her father left the house. Then for weeks, we slept together in my queen-sized bed, more for my sake than hers, me feeling so left and bereft and crazed, I didn't know how to be the grown-up, not acknowledging that her father had left her, too. Gabi heard me crying late at night and came into my bed. She rubbed my back, spoke soothingly, told me everything was going to be all right. I wanted to believe her, knowing there was an oddness to this, the tables turning, the child coming to comfort the mother in the dark. The next night we read together for a while, and when I turned off the light, she remained. It was kind of nice spending the night together, both of us sad to the core. Gabi and I shared the bed for a couple of weeks. Once, turning out the light, she said, "You know, maybe some people would think this sleeping together is a little weird, but we won't do it forever."

For my forty-second birthday, the same year of my divorce from her father, Gabi gave me a nightgown. The Sheep Nightgown, we ended up calling it. The sheep nightgown is soft flannel, baby blue and white, with row after row of plump sheep on impossibly skinny legs. Powder blue stars dot the background.

"I love it," I had told her, immediately getting undressed and putting the nightgown over my head. By then, she was no longer sleeping in my bed. I had a new job, was seeing a therapist, was starting to see Joe who became my husband. But those first few months of sleeping alone were spent almost exclusively in the sheep nightgown. I made tea with a shot of bourbon, took a book to bed, propped the phone on my shoulder and talked with friends late into the night. Before turning off the light I would feel comforted by those sweet, silly sheep.

The sheep nightgown held up over many washings. A coffee stain came out with a presoak. To protect the fabric, I stopped putting the nightgown in the dryer. Eventually, I put the nightgown away, but it emerges every now and then, when I have a flu, or on the odd times when Joe is out of town, and the Iowa winds make lonely howls.

I don't remember much that first night in the hospital, but I was awake enough to know how badly I had to urinate. Once you are up in the night and have to pee, it's over. You have to get up. Even if you are hooked up to monitors and IVs and are not even twenty-four hours out of surgery. I saw Gabi sleeping peacefully on her cot; so deciding not to wake her, I inched myself to the edge of the bed, carefully swung my feet over and felt for the floor. Slowly standing—everything on my body seemed so tight, it was hard to get upright—I took a shaky, deep breath. The IV was bulky and the wheels squeaked as I took a step. Suddenly Gabi sat bolt upright on her cot: "Mom, what the hell are you doing?"

"I didn't want to wake you," I said.

"You are impossible," she told me, pulling back her cover. "Don't move." She got up and began to steer me in the direction of the bathroom. She smelled like herself, like Gabi, in the middle of the night.

Joe's log recorded that a few of our doctor friends came by that first day, so the nurses on the floor must have been surprised to see a gynecologist, an allergist, and an ophthalmologist, sitting bedside and chatting with him, as I drifted in and out of sleep. My internist, Rupal Amin came, too. I remember her bending by the side of the bed, caressing my arm, her voice hushed.

Gabi went home and took a shower and came back with a chocolate Butterfinger Blizzard from Dairy Queen. "How did you know what I wanted?" I asked when I awoke. "No, you're only allowed clear broths," she told me, but laughed when I made her share.

On Tuesday afternoon, the day after the operation, they began to unhook me from the monitors and IV. People were calling, but I didn't want anyone to come. "I'll be home tomorrow," I said. Along with my no-floral dictum, I told my friends that I didn't want visitors. I meant it, too. There's something humiliating about being captive with bed-head and hospital pallor. Not to mention a bandaged flat chest. Below chin level, I looked like a young girl. When Mark Taylor came by that evening and asked if I was "ready" to have a look, I said, "Sure." Gabi was standing bedside.

"Are you going to be all right?" Mark asked, hesitating before he peeled away some of the dressing. Maybe the drugs caused a certain medical detachment, but I didn't feel emotional about the unveiling. Did he anticipate that seeing myself, my breasts gone, I would cry or fall apart? No, I was prepared for this. I've been a child who saw her grandmother's scarred chest in our apartment in the Bronx. I had helped my mother get ready for bed after her mastectomy in Florida. All summer I had studied photographs of breastless chests on the FORCE website.

"Are you ready?" Mark Taylor asked, as he pulled back the bandages.

Of course, I was ready. I have been ready all my life.

23

Her search revealed a sisterhood of women with hereditary breast and ovarian cancer (HBOC), sharing their advice, knowledge, and experience. Kupfer chose to have two separate operations: an oophorectomy (removal of the ovaries and fallopian tubes) and a double mastectomy. Both are prophylactic surgeries to prevent a future cancer diagnosis.

(Medical Center Newsletter)

So there it was, a gigantic photograph on a billboard on the corner of Duff and Lincoln Way, probably the busiest intersection in Ames. In this picture, I am smiling, leaning over the railing on my backyard deck, amid colorful clay pots of flowers. A friend called to tell me about it. "Jeez, Fern, I almost drove right into the car in front of me," she said. "What are you doing on a billboard?"

Oh, yeah, I had forgotten about that. In early the summer, sometime before the mastectomies, Mary Ellen from the hospital cancer clinic called and asked if I would give permission for a reporter to interview me about the experience of genetic testing. "Telling your story could really help other women," she had said. "Many people just don't know. And some women are reluctant to talk about this." She believed that I would not be among the reluctant. "Sure," I said.

The next thing I knew, a photographer came to the house, posing me in the backyard, snapping away from all angles as if I were a runway model. "That's it. Smile. Smile," he urged. I thought of an old Julie Christie movie where the photographer keeps saying, "Happy girl, happy girl."

The same week, a woman who had been a student in my magazine writing class at the university years before, met me at Stomping Grounds for the interview. "Come with questions," I had told the class about preparing for an interview, "but don't feel as if you have to stick to the script. It's your responsibility to make sure that the person you are interviewing is relaxed into having a real conversation." She was a little nervous to show me the final copy. "I'm sure it will be very professional," I told her. But I didn't know it was going to be the lead story, so I was surprised when the medical center magazine came out with an 8 by 10 color glossy of me on the cover and the dramatic headline: *Powerful Knowledge. How genetic testing may have saved an Ames woman's life.* Well, that's a hook.

This magazine, published four times a year, is mailed to everyone in town who has ever received the services of the Mary Greeley Medical Center. Which is practically everyone. People I didn't even know stopped me in the street to tell me how brave I was to "share my story." When I went to pick up my mail at school, colleagues came up to me: "How *are* you?" they asked with concern.

Mary Ellen called again soon after the magazine came out with another question. Would I also give permission to use that cover photo for a billboard, advertising the medical clinic? I agreed. The billboard would also be a promotion of sorts for using the medical services here in Ames. *Good care, close to home,* it said in letters six feet tall beside my cheery photo.

And home was where I was after only two days in the hospital following the removal of both of my breasts. Friends came by with books and lemon tarts; Cynthia sent make-up and facial moisturizer; Mary Beth, away at her lake house for August, sent trinkets every day for a week—stuff she found at garage sales up in Minnesota. Gabi flew home to Chicago, and Katie arrived in Iowa. Apron clad, she and Joe cooked together in the kitchen, filling the house up with the smells of lamb, garlic, cinnamon and allspice.

Mark Taylor, my surgeon, made a house call to check the drains and dressing. *Good care, close to home,* especially if your husband plays poker with the doctors. Mark is probably over six and a half feet tall, but he seemed even larger in my bedroom, looming over the side of the bed. One of the tubes in my chest was draining more readily than the other. There were two of these inserted into the chest wall running the pus and gook into a little vial which fit neatly into a pocket on the cotton camisole given to me by the clinic. One of the tubes was stopped up, so Mark cleaned it out. "That's the side I had some trouble with," he said, affirming that there would have been more difficulty had I chosen to begin reconstruction during the surgery. I had "poor vascularity," he said. Vascularity. The vascular system is the way blood travels through the body, and includes the arteries and capillaries. I wasn't sure what having "poor" vascularity meant, but it didn't sound like something anyone should want while spending time under the knife.

After five days I went to Mark's office, and he removed one of the drains. Then, a few days later, I went back, and he took out the next one. My chest still hurt, but I was thrilled to be free of the disgusting drains. It reminded me of a Yiddish folk tale my mother had loved: *Too Much Noise*, the story of a poor peasant who is driven crazy living with a wife and many children in a small hut. The wise Rabbi suggests that the man take in his mother-in-law, then a barnyard full of animals. "What?!!" responds the man. Adding clucking chickens and *kvetching* in-laws made even more noise. It was only after the hut was eventually emptied of the additions that the man was grateful for the condition that he had previously complained about. His home seemed quiet in comparison. So it was after I was free of the drains that I felt happy with only a tightly smocked chest.

The first week Nancy came over and planted a year-round hibiscus on the west side of the house. My son-in-law, Bill, sent ten pints of gourmet ice cream from Homer's in Chicago. I took Vicodin and read book after book on the front porch glider. Barbara flew in, and, good to her promise, behaved in as low-key a way as Barbara possibly could, reading with me on the porch. The mailman, who had seen my face on the hundreds of hospital newsletters he had delivered, looked in every now and then to ask how I was doing.

After about three weeks, I went back to the clinic for Mark to take out the last of the stitches and in the waiting room saw my neighbor, Jean, a retired voice teacher. Jean is one of those ultra nice, glass-half-full people, who had survived a virulent breast cancer many years ago; she still has trouble with lymphedema, a fluid obstruction that causes pain and swelling of the arm. "Fern, dear, it's so nice to see you," she said, her voice rising melodically. She told me how good I looked so soon after the surgery, how lucky I was because now I would not get breast cancer. "Good, for you," she declared. "For making that decision." Also, she had seen me on the billboard.

She was going for a check-up before heading off on some adventure. She and her husband are volunteer park rangers, on the lookout for forest fires in remote national parks. I have known Jean for years, but it was only at that moment, talking with her, that I looked at her chest, realizing that she was flat-chested, unreconstructed and wearing no prosthetics. We talked about that. "I have to remember to just stand straight," she said, pushing back her shoulders as if she were about to conduct an orchestra.

"How's the range of motion?" Mark asked, when I entered his office. Joe followed and took the side chair.

"Good," I said, trying to be a compliant non-complainer, after my chat with Jean. "I'm pretty good."

Still taking the pain pills?" he asked. I had cut down on the Vicodin, before totally running out the day before. I asked Mark for another prescription just because it made me nervous not to have any back-up at all. "I won't take advantage," I promised.

"Ok," he allowed. "But watch it." He looked at Joe as if to remind him that I should watch it. Some doctors are more wary of prescription remedies than others. Mark seems the tough-it-out type. Dr. Amin suggests I do deep-breathing exercises and meditation. Tim Leeds says, take the pills if you need them.

"So let's see how you're doing," Mark said wheeling a chair up to the examination table. "This looks good," he said. "You're healing nicely." Where my breasts had been were two identical arcs, like frowns carved onto a jack-o-lantern. Eight black stitches on either side created the scary teeth. Mark clipped the last of the stitches. "Looks really good," he said again, admiring his handiwork.

"Yeah, you think?" I said, sighing.

One night, Tim and his wife brought over supper and we played Scrabble, Tim gloating when I didn't win. "No handicaps for you," he said, triumphantly putting down a seven letter word. I hadn't known it before, but found out that Tim had actually come into the operating room, called there by Mark Taylor for a consultation right in the middle of performing my mastectomies. Because of the poor vascularity there was a chance of losing a skin flap on one side. The outcome wouldn't look quite as good, would not be quite symmetrical. To make it "perfect," however, he could perform a follow-up procedure.

Mark called Tim, because Tim knew me better than he did. Was I a perfectionist? What if the outcome would not be as cosmetically successful? Tim was sure: Just do what is necessary and finish up. "Believe me, you don't want to have to see Fern again. Just go ahead," he told Mark.

"So you were both standing over my bloody chest and discussing how I would respond to this?" I asked Tim. I thought of Elaine on Seinfeld. "Difficult patient," had been written on her medical chart and followed her everywhere. There was a part of Tim that I knew felt proud. Because Mark himself was a perfectionist. He was someone who usually had the answers, not the questions.

"Well, I was right, wasn't I?" Tim said.

I told him that he was.

It has taken some getting used to, but if I had to do it over again, I would do the same thing. Getting the genetic testing. Moving quickly. Having both the oophorectomy and the mastectomies. Having both operations in Ames, *so close to home.*

And yes, even choosing not to have any reconstruction. I know this isn't the right choice for everyone, and in all honesty, there are times that I believe it was not absolutely right for me. I'm vain. I like clothes. Since the operation I have sometimes emerged from a shower, looked in the mirror at my scarred chest and envisioned two synthetically rounded globes. Just throw on a tank top and be ready to go. I take a handful of belly-fat and imagine it gone, placed where breasts would be. Then I remember intensive surgery, intensive care. Or living with something foreign (silicone), being uncomfortable, unable to take off. Ever. If I knew reconstruction would be easy and uncomplicated, I would have done it. But nothing ever is.

Not having breasts has been mostly an annoyance, not a devastation. I don't, as my cousin predicted, "feel maimed." Or certainly less like me. I think of breasts now as a fashion accessory. I go flat around the house. Flat in cold weather, wearing a scarf and a vest when I go out. It's just more comfortable that way. I have alternate sizes of falsies for different occasions. If I'm wearing a snug turtleneck. If I'm wearing a silk blouse. A bathing suit. I have prostheses that the insurance paid for which were over seven hundred dollars. I have some I picked up at Target for $5.98 which work perfectly well. So do, recalling my junior high days, cut-up nylon stockings. The fact is, no one is looking all that closely at me. My mom used to tell me that when I was a self-conscious teenager, agonizing about what to wear the first day of school. "Everyone's just thinking about themselves, Fernie," she said. "No one's looking that hard at you."

I really don't feel less of a woman. I wear a pretty teddy when Joe and I make love. I am the one he wants, always. And he thinks that even for an old broad with no breasts, that I am still a hot number.

Prophylactic surgeries prevent a future cancer diagnosis, the hospital magazine said. But there's nothing to say there wouldn't be a cancer of the lung, lying in wait from my college smoking days. Nothing to ensure that a melanoma wouldn't appear, a result of teenage summers baking under the delicious sun at Jones Beach.

Having survived this far, I know that despite trying to live wisely and make judicious, well-researched decisions, there is nothing to prevent a drunk from flying through a stop-sign and t-boning the Toyota. There are no money-back guarantees for an extension on this life. Just as there is no assurance that the infant delivered from your young, perfect body would be a little boy who had all the enzymes necessary to make him perfect and whole. Also there are no promises that the husband you married at twenty-one, who vowed to love and cherish and be faithful to you until death do you part, would be the same man you would eventually grow old with.

In the autumn of every year, there is "rush," a rite of passage where the girls just out of high school attend parties at the sorority houses. The Big Sisters welcome the new pledges with enthusiastic cheers; popular songs have lyrics altered to meet the needs of the Chi Omegas or the Sigma Kappas. When new girls are inducted there are solemn hymns and candle-lighting ceremonies; the air is still heavy with late summer heat, the lines of girls are wobbly on their high heels; their golden tans have not yet faded.

The semester before I retired, a student came to my office and told me that she was applying for teaching jobs in Chicago. She knew I was leaving, but would I please write her a recommendation? Tall and blond like many of my Iowa students—she was familiar enough for me to recall her in class the year before. I was pleased that I even remembered her name: Kimberly. I had three girls named Kimberly that semester. She was Kimberly T.

"I've always loved your office," she said. The office was decorated in mauves and soft greens, with lacy curtains, a faux fireplace, an oriental rug and family pictures on the bookshelves.

It is a homey nook. Kimberly T. handed me an envelope for the recommendation and her resume. I recalled that she did her work, probably got a B, is a nice person who loves children. She will make an earnest and dedicated teacher.

Although it is not like when I graduated from college in 1968 when all the smart Long Island girls were going to be teachers. My mother had told me that teaching was a great profession for a woman. I could work and still be home in time to make dinner for my husband.

Shyly, Kimberly T. showed me her left hand where a small diamond sparkled. "Next summer," she said proudly. She and her fiancée were saving for a wedding and applying for jobs in Chicago. She shared that she had never lived anywhere but Iowa and felt nervous about "city life."

I assured her that she would do fine, wishing her luck on getting a teaching job, congratulating her on the impending marriage. She thanked me again, telling me how much she enjoyed my class. Standing in the doorway, filled with hopeful anticipation, she added: "And, seriously, I really learned a lot."

Me too, I have to say. Learned a lot is the benefit of being over sixty years old. In the many decades since I have left Long Island this is what I know: that life is fragile and exquisite; that the evil eye is chancy and capricious; that personal pain can be a means of grace, the way to find your truest, most capable self. And that as long as you're alive and walking around with your eyes open—nothing, almost nothing, is finished or forever.

Acknowledgements

Thanks to those who have been there: the help offered by the FORCE website, the women who met me for coffee, emailed, who spoke with me in the night. Most especially, I am indebted to Diana Elliott, whose brave and determined spirit was nothing short of inspiring.

I am grateful to live in a community of caring medical professionals who are also friends, especially Tim Leeds, Mark Taylor, Ken Talbert, John Paschen and Jay Brown.

Thank you cousin Charmian and Jon Weber for generosity beyond bounds. To cousin Linda for empathy without judgment. And to my brother, Ray, who always loves me no matter what.

Thanks to my editor, Mikesch Muecke, for his enthusiasm and expertise. And to Steve Mumford for his confidence and resourcefulness in publicity. This has been great fun!

Thanks to encouraging readers and friends: Joanne Brown, Jamie Horwitz, Andi Smith, Nancy St. Clair and Jane Zaring.

Thanks to Michael Rakosi—you know why.

My girls, Katie, Megan and Gabi, are wise and savvy editors. Thank you for putting up with a "writer-mom" all these years and for good-naturedly letting me share your stories as well my own.

Living with a writer is a blessing. How can I thank my husband for reading and rereading, for keeping me well-fed and well-loved? And for reading once again. No, Joe Geha, I am the lucky one.

Made in the USA
Middletown, DE
03 May 2022

65197224R00156